MW01283480

Fighting for the SOUL of your Child

A PRACTICAL GUIDE TO BIBLICAL PARENTING

JIMMY & KAREN EVANS
JULIE EVANS ALBRACHT

XO
PUBLISHING

CONTENTS

Section 1: Rules of Engagement

Section 2: Boot Camp

Section 3: Battlefields

Meet the Authors

JIMMY & KAREN EVANS founded MarriageToday (now called XO Marriage) in 1994 to help couples thrive in strong and fulfilling marriages. Together, they hosted *MarriageToday with Jimmy and Karen*, a television show and ministry designed to bring hope and healing to hurting couples. Jimmy has written more than 50 books including *Marriage on the Rock, The Four Laws of Love, 21 Day Inner Healing Journey*, and *Tipping Point*. Karen is the author of *From Pain to Paradise*. Jimmy and Karen have been married for 50 years and have two married children and five grandchildren.

JULIE EVANS ALBRACHT is the daughter of Jimmy and Karen Evans. She and her husband, Cory, have been married 27 years and have adult twin daughters named Elle and Abby. This is Julie's second book to work on with her father. Julie had the concept idea for *Where Are the Missing People?*, a post-Rapture guide for those left behind. Jimmy and Julie also had a podcast called *Standing for Truth*. Julie and Cory reside in the Texas Hill Country where Julie lives out her love and passion as an interior designer, alongside her desire to share a life lived from a biblical perspective.

Foreword

At the heart of this book, *Fighting for the Soul of Your Child*, is a wealth of wisdom and insight I've known the Evans family for a long time, and they have such a passion for building strong, healthy, and godly marriages and families. The information you are about to read will give you a deeper revelation of your role as a parent and will equip you with tools and strategies to maximize your impact in every phase of your child's life. From understanding the four basic needs of a child to instilling a strong value system and beyond, you'll find a treasure trove of wisdom that will help to enrich your relationship with your child while aiding them in becoming the person God created them to be. This book is a must read for every parent and grandparent. Remember, we are all on a journey to eternity, and you have more influence on your children than you may realize. So set good boundaries to keep them safe, encourage their uniqueness, show them a tangible representation of God's love, and never stop believing for all that God has purposed for their life.

Joni Lamb
Daystar Television Network

WElcOME

The book you have just opened has been a project of firsts. It's the first time we (Jimmy and Karen) have written a full-length book together. It's the first time our daughter, Julie, has joined us as a coauthor. And it's the first time XO Marriage (formerly MarriageToday) has released a book dedicated to the topic of parenting.

Now you might be wondering, *I thought Jimmy and Karen were the marriage people?* It's true, we have said a lot about marriage over the past three decades. In 1993, God gave me (Jimmy) the vision for what would be for the largest marriage-focused ministry in the world. Through our books, podcasts, conferences, and *MarriageToday* television program, we have helped millions of couples discover that when you do marriage God's way, you have a 100 percent chance of success.

In addition to marriage, I (Jimmy) have taken a deep dive into the topic of the end times. Perhaps you've seen *Tipping Point with Jimmy Evans* on YouTube or heard our weekly podcast. Maybe you read one of my end times books (*Tipping Point*, *Where Are the Missing People?*, or *Look Up!*). I am passionate about this topic because I truly believe we are living in the last days. Some people are fearful because they don't know what to expect, and they aren't sure they're ready for whatever "it" is. I'm here to tell you that you don't have to be afraid. You can know exactly what to expect, and you can be fully prepared. God has never abandoned His people, and He's not going to abandon you either.

Why Did We Write a Parenting Book?

In 1947, Harvard sociologist Carle Zimmerman released a report called *Family and Civilization*.[1] In his report, he warned that America was liberalizing our family laws and policies much like former world empires that fell from within (Rome, Egypt, Babylon, Greece, etc.). Zimmerman named some signs that preceded the fall of each of those empires. The first sign in every case was that marriage lost its sacredness. After that, companionate forms of marriage (cohabitation) arose, women lost their inclination for childbearing (falling birth rates), children began to rebel against their parents, juvenile delinquency skyrocketed, and immorality became rampant.

Every single sign that preceded the fall of each empire from within is present in America today and is getting worse. For the purposes of this book, let's look at some research on marriage, single-parenting, and birth rates in the United States.

Marriage

- "Only 44% of Millennials were married in 2019."[2]

- "The share of adults ages 25 to 54 who are currently married fell from 67% in 1990 to 53% in 2019, while the share cohabiting more than doubled over that same period (from 4% in 1990 to 9% in 2019)."[3]

- "The share who have never been married has also grown—from 17% to 33%."[4]

Single-Parenting

- "A new Pew Research Center study of 130 countries and territories shows that the U.S. has the world's highest rate of children living in single-parent households."[5]

- "Almost a quarter of U.S. children under the age of 18 live with one parent and no other adults (23%), more than three times the share of children around the world who do so (7%)."[6]

- "The share of U.S. children living with an unmarried parent has more than doubled since 1968, jumping from 13% to 32% in 2017."[7]

Birth Rates

- "Forty-three states recorded their lowest general fertility rate, which represents annual births per 1,000 women aged 15–44, in at least three decades in 2020."[8]

- "44% of non-parents ages 18 to 49 say it is not too or not at all likely that they will have children someday, an increase of 7 percentage points from the 37% who said the same in a 2018 survey."[9]

- "A majority (56%) of non-parents younger than 50 who say it's unlikely they will have children someday say they just don't want to have kids. Childless adults younger than 40 are more likely to say this than those ages 40 to 49 (60% vs. 46%, respectively)."[10]

Now, please do not misunderstand—we are not sharing these findings to condemn anyone. We applaud every man and woman who believes in the sanctity of life and recognizes that a baby growing inside the womb is a person, not just a blob of tissue. And whether you are a single mom or a single dad, being the solo parent is an enormous responsibility, and we pray blessings over you and your family.

Why Is This Parenting Book Important Today?

The undeniable truth is staring us in the face: there is an attack on everything the Bible says and everything traditional societies have held sacred. Paul warned this would happen when he wrote about "the coming of our Lord Jesus Christ":

> For that day will not come until there is a great rebellion against God and the man of lawlessness is revealed—the one who brings destruction. He will exalt himself and defy everything that people call god and every object of worship. He will even sit in the temple of God, claiming that he himself is God (2 Thessalonians 2:3–4 NLT).

The sign the apostle Paul gave to indicate that we were living in the days just prior to Christ's return has come true. For those of us who are believers, this means we need to be strong and not bow our knees to the pressures that are in the world to compromise our beliefs. Even though we should never be self-righteous or mean-spirited, we must be vigilant to stand for Jesus and the Bible. We aren't fighting against people who disagree with our beliefs; we are battling an antichrist spirit that is announcing the approaching arrival of the lawless one—the Antichrist himself.

As parents, we do not have the right or the time to be complacent when it comes to our kids. Psalm 127:3 says, "Children are a gift from the LORD; they are a reward from him" (NLT). It is our responsibility as Christ-followers to love, protect, and steward this gift for the glory of God. Here are two Scripture passages we will examine repeatedly throughout this book:

> Train up a child in the way he should go,
> And when he is old he will not depart from it (Proverbs 22:6).

> And you must commit yourselves wholeheartedly to these commands that I am giving you today. Repeat them again and again to your children. Talk about them when you are at home and when you are on the road, when you are going to bed and when you are getting up. Tie them to your hands and wear them on your forehead as reminders. Write them on the doorposts of your house and on your gates (Deuteronomy 6:6–9 NLT).

This book is for parents of all ages and stages. Are you thinking about having kids? Many people do some form of premarital counseling, but few do pre-parental training. This book, paired with Scripture, will be a roadmap to raising up children with biblical principles.

> Before I formed you in the womb, I knew you; before you were born I set you apart (Jeremiah 1:5 NIV).

Are your children acting defiant and mischievous? No matter what any parent on social media may claim, no one has a perfect child. This book will help you learn how to stop fighting *with* your child and start fighting *for* them instead.

> For we are not fighting against flesh-and-blood enemies, but against evil rulers and authorities of the unseen world, against mighty powers in this dark world, and against evil spirits in the heavenly places (Ephesians 6:12 NLT).

Are you concerned about today's culture war and its effects on your kids? The enemy wants to steal, kill, and destroy the family unit (see John 10:10), and he will use every means at his disposal. This book will teach you how to recognize Satan's schemes and combat them with the authority of God's Word and the practicality of godly wisdom.

> The weapons we fight with are not the weapons of the world. On the contrary, they have divine power to demolish strongholds. We demolish arguments and every pretension that sets itself up against the knowledge of God, and we take captive every thought to make it obedient to Christ (2 Corinthians 10:4–5).

Why Did We Write This Book Together?

We (Jimmy and Karen) have had the privilege to counsel parents from all walks of life for 40-plus years, and I (Jimmy) have been teaching on Bible-based parenting almost as long. If we haven't seen it all by now, then we've definitely seen most of it! Yes, there have been plenty of surface-level changes over the years, particularly with technology and social media, but the core issue of humanity remains the same. Every person deals with sin, and sin has a negative effect on everything we do.

You don't have to be a child "expert" to realize that raising the next generation to be decent, God-fearing people is a challenging task. Every parent makes mistakes, and that includes us. We weren't (and aren't) perfect parents by any means, as you will discover in the stories ahead. Through some hard-fought lessons, we learned the pain of parenting our own way, but we also discovered the incredible blessings that come from parenting God's way. Today, we have the sweetest joy of seeing our children and grandchildren love the Lord and serve Him with all their hearts.

The Evans family has grown from our original family unit of four to eleven wonderfully imperfect people. We believe what God's Word says about life, and with the help of the Holy Spirit, we abide by it daily. I (Julie) have two daughters in college, and as empty nesters, my husband and I are in a new season of parenting young adults. It's definitely been an adjustment, but it would have been even more challenging without the work we did when they were young.

We (Jimmy and Karen) have been empty nesters for longer than we care to admit, but we absolutely love being grandparents. If children are a gift from the Lord, then grandchildren are bonus prizes! By the way, we are so proud of Julie and our son, Brent. There were plenty of difficult days when Brent and Jimmy butted heads, and Julie and Karen couldn't seem to agree on anything. You'll read about some of those days in this book. But God gave our family everything we needed. As we submitted our lives to Him, He was faithful to carry us through even the darkest times. He gave us wisdom at just the right moments and showered us with boundless grace. He'll do the same for you if you'll just ask Him.

Job 8:8 says, "Ask the former generation and find out what their ancestors learned" (NIV). There is wisdom in learning from those who have gone before you. I (Julie) continue to learn from my parents every day. We may not agree on every single issue and situation, but we agree on the most important details: God gave us His Word, and when our families live by it, we have a 100 percent chance of happiness and success.

We realize that *Fighting for the Soul of Your Child* is a serious title. It may even be a bit uncomfortable. And it's sure to evoke some questions:

- What is the soul?
- Why do I need to fight for it?
- What kind of battlefields will I be fighting on?

We promise to answer these questions and many more throughout the pages of this book. We want you to be armed with all the information you need (and probably more than you wanted!) to raise up godly kids. Of course, we're not saying that we have all the answers. The three of us have made plenty of mistakes, and we're sure we will make plenty more. There's only one perfect Father. But He didn't leave us alone. He gave us the perfect Guidebook (His Word) and the perfect Guide (the Holy Spirit).

Speaking of the Holy Spirit, Jesus said, "When the Spirit of truth comes, he will guide you into all truth" (John 16:13 NLT). We are going to share some difficult things with you in this book. You won't like every verse, fact, and statistic, and you might find yourself wanting to put the book down and slowly back away. We understand. Would it be easier to stay in bed, pull the sheets up over our heads, and hide from this crazy world? Sure, it would. But our kids need us. They need us to be men and women of faith who will rise up, put on our spiritual armor, and go to war for them. Their future depends on it.

Jesus said, "You will know the truth, and the truth will set you free" (John 8:32 NLT). Fear not, friends. Let us go forward and fight!

SECTION 1

RULES OF ENGAGEMENT

1

THE GREATER PURPOSE

What is your purpose as a parent? It's a big question, we know, especially when many people are still trying to figure out their purpose as an individual. A quick internet search for "purpose as a parent" offers *1.7 billion* results, with phrases like "good values," "unconditional love," "functional adults," and "positive impact on society." Obviously, there are plenty of opinions about parenting, but which one is the right one?

In January 2023, Pew Research Center released a study of thousands of parents across the United States from various ethnicities and income levels. One topic addressed by the study was parenting priorities:

> When asked about their aspirations for their children when they reach adulthood, parents prioritize financial independence and career satisfaction. Roughly nine-in-ten parents say it's extremely or very important to them that their children be financially independent when they are adults, and the same share say it's equally important that their children have jobs or careers they enjoy.[1]

These parents are concerned about financial independence and career satisfaction for their children. In other words, they want their kids to be successful and happy.

And isn't that what everyone wants? The three of us don't know any sane, healthy parents who actively root for their children to be *un*happy and *un*successful. Of course, methods differ when it comes to these parenting goals. Some parents gently encourage and nudge, while others firmly push and prod. There are parents who only think about their children's happiness: "I don't care what Jared grows up to be, as long as he's happy doing it." There are parents who believe success is paramount to everything else: "The reason I push Sarah so hard in school because I want her to be successful in her future career." And, of course, there are parents who want their kids to have it all.

But are happiness and success really *all* there is? And if so, what happens when your children are not happy or not successful? Because those times will happen. In spite of your best efforts, you will not always be able to manage your child's emotions or manipulate their life experiences. They will be sad sometimes. They will struggle sometimes. And sometimes, they will flat out fail. What happens then?

There has to be something *more*. There has to be a greater purpose to parenting. And there has to be a way to accomplish this greater purpose.

The Human Purpose

The Bible holds the answers to life's biggest questions, and parenting is no exception. Before we look at the purpose of parenting, however, we need to look at what the Bible says about the purpose of every individual. (Spoiler alert: it's not to be happy or successful.)

> Hear, O Israel: The LORD our God, the LORD is one! You shall love the LORD your God with all your heart, with all your soul, and with all your strength (Deuteronomy 6:4–5).

Jesus confirms this command in Matthew chapter 22:

Then one of them, a lawyer, asked *Him a question*, testing Him, and saying, "Teacher, which *is* the great commandment in the law?"

Jesus said to him, "'You shall love the LORD your God with all your heart, with all your soul, and with all your mind.' This is *the* first and great commandment" (vv. 35–38).[2]

These verses are clear: we are commanded to love God. (In the next chapter, we will talk about what it means to love the Lord "with all your soul.")

An essential part of loving God is knowing Him. After all, you can't really love someone you don't know. People all over the world claim to "love" celebrities they've never met, but this is really infatuation based on the limited amount of information made available to the public. In order to truly love a person, you have to know more than what they do, what they wear, and what causes they support. You have to know the real *them*. Therefore, to love God, you have to know the real Him. And to know Him, you have to spend time with Him on a daily basis.

An essential part of loving God is knowing Him.

Many people have a distorted view of God, which makes it difficult to love Him. You can only get as close to God as your concept of Him will allow. Here are three things every person needs to know:

God Is Good

We are here to tell you that *God is a good God.* In Genesis chapter 1, He created the earth and everything in it, and He placed the first humans, Adam and Eve, in a beautiful garden. Then Satan, in the form of a serpent, slithered into the garden and started hissing lies about God. Once Adam and Eve believed these poisonous concepts, they sinned. Then, to make matters worse, they hid in shame because they evidently did not believe God would forgive them (see Genesis 3:1–5).

Even though God is nothing like Satan said, many times we find it easier to believe a lie than to accept the truth. Most of us develop our first concepts of God from our parents as we grow up. It's great if children have generous, loving, and kind parents, because they tend to view God as generous, loving, and kind. But if children have distant, uncaring, legalistic, or abusive parents, then they tend to think of God in those terms.

When I (Jimmy) was growing up, I played lots of different sports, but my dad never came to a single game. I invited him all the time, but he just wasn't involved in my day-to-day life. I felt like my dad didn't really know me, so when I became a Christian at the age of 19, I had a difficult time believing that God knew me either. I struggled to trust Him with every part of my life. But over time, I realized that God was good and *only* good. He always kept His promises, He always provided, and He never once turned His back on me.

God Is Loving

The Bible says, "Perfect love casts out fear ... We love Him because He first loved us" (1 John 4:18–19). God's perfect love will heal your heart. He wants to do a magnificent work in your life because He loves you. We heard one preacher say it this way: "God loves you just the way you are, but He also loves you too much to let you stay that way."

In New Testament Greek, there's a unique word that speaks of God's love: *agape*. *Agape* is the only expression of love that doesn't require an emotion. Yes, God has emotions, but His love doesn't require it, because He *is* love. First John 4:8 says, "He who does not love does not know God, for God is love." Likewise, when Jesus tells us to love our neighbors as ourselves in Mark 12:31, this is *agape*. It doesn't matter how we feel about our neighbors—our emotions are not in the driver's seat. We choose to love them the same way God chooses to love us.

I (Karen) have been a Christian for more than 50 years, but for many of those years, it was incredibly hard to believe that God loved me. When I was growing up, my brother told me *every single day*, "You're so stupid. You're so fat. You're so ugly." Self-hate became such a big part of who I was that when I read verses like John 3:16 ("For God so loved the world ..."), I thought, *Well, God loves everyone else, but He only likes me. And I understand why You don't love me, Lord—I'm not easy to love.* I wanted to believe what the Bible said, but it took years of spending time in God's Word *every single day* to discover that God wasn't like the men in my family. He really, truly loves me exactly as I am. His love healed my heart and made me a new person.

God Is Gracious

The Lord is good, even when you don't deserve His goodness. He loves you even when everyone else thinks you're unlovable. Even so, the enemy works full-time to convince you that God's acceptance of you is based on a point system. If you're doing well, then you "deserve" God's favor, but if you're not doing well, then you deserve His wrath.

The truth is that every person deserves God's wrath. In Romans 3:23, the apostle Paul wrote, "For all have sinned and fall short of the glory of God" (NIV). We would have no hope, if not for verse 24: "And all are justified freely by his grace through the redemption that came by Christ Jesus" (NIV). Jesus took your place on the cross and took the punishment for your sins. If you receive Him by faith, the curse of sin is forever removed from your life. Ephesians 2:8–9 says, "For by grace you have been saved through faith, and that not of yourselves; *it is* the gift of God, not of works, lest anyone should boast."

When Jesus came to earth, He faced the same temptations and problems you experience. He is your sympathetic High Priest (see Hebrews 4:15), and because of Him, you can go to God and say, "I'm really hurting and struggling. Please help me." God will not respond to you with legalism or judgment. He won't tell you that you make Him sick or that He's tired of you. No, you can "come boldly to the throne of grace, that [you] may obtain mercy and find grace to help in time of need" (Hebrews 4:16). What an amazing promise!

The Parent Purpose

We've established that your purpose as an individual is to know and love God. Now, let's look at what the Bible says about your purpose as a parent.

> Therefore you shall lay up these words of mine in your heart and in your soul, and bind them as a sign on your hand, and they shall be as frontlets between your eyes. You shall teach them to your children, speaking of them when you sit in your house, when you walk by the way, when you lie down, and when you rise up. And you shall write them on the doorposts of your house and on your gates, that your days and the days of your children may be multiplied in the land of which the LORD swore to your fathers to give them, like the days of the heavens above the earth (Deuteronomy 11:18–21).

> Train up a child in the way he should go,
> And when he is old he will not depart from it (Proverbs 22:6).

> And you, fathers, do not provoke your children to wrath, but bring them up in the training and admonition of the Lord (Ephesians 6:4).

According to these verses, **your greater purpose as a parent is to teach and train your child to know and love God.** This is your mission, your chief assignment.

Now, every child has four basic needs: acceptance, identity, security, and purpose. These needs are incredibly important for every person, and ultimately, they can only be completely satisfied by knowing and loving God. As adults, we are able to establish a personal relationship with Jesus and our spouses in order to find the deep, inner satisfaction that we need. However, although our children can accept Christ and love Him at a young age, having their needs met during the first 18 years of their lives is largely dependent upon us. We are their protectors and providers, and as such, we play a critical role in meeting these basic needs as we teach and train our children. We will talk more about these needs in the next chapter.

Your greater purpose as a parent is to teach and train your child to know and love God.

Teaching and training are often used interchangeably in our culture, but there is important meaning behind both words. In Deuteronomy 11, parents are told to teach their children God's commands by "speaking of them" four specific times: when you are at home, when you are traveling somewhere, when you are going to bed, and when you wake up in the morning. That just about covers an entire day, doesn't it? I (Julie) have twin daughters with my husband, Cory, and every day, we made it a parenting goal to point our family conversations back to the Bible. It didn't matter how big or small the topic was. We always wanted our girls to know what God's Word said so that they would be successfully prepared for life.

In Proverbs 22:6, the word "train" comes from the Hebrew word *chanak*, which means 'to put something into the mouth.' Pulpit Commentary offers this picture: "To give to be tasted as nurses give to infants food which they have masticated in order to prepare it for their nurslings."[3] In other words, an adult would pre-chew the food and then put it in the infant's mouth, thus demonstrating the way to eat. When you train a child, you aren't simply talking. Yes, you are telling them something, but you are also living that something in front of them. "Sit there and watch me, and I'm going to train you how to do it."

Understanding this dual teaching and training purpose changes the way you relate to your children. No longer are you simply doing what your parents did because they were "good parents" or not doing what your parents did because they were "bad parents." You are parenting on purpose—there is a divine *why* behind everything you do. When parents don't know the why, they tend to be weak, inconsistent, reactive, and sometimes even hopeless. But parents who know the why are confident, consistent, proactive, and strong even in hard times.

Parents are the image-bearers of God to their children and the filter by which their children view God. Do you want to your child to know and love God because of your behavior or in spite of it? We must remember that God is the Creator of the family. Therefore, only His purpose will empower us to raise our children properly. Parenting takes tremendous faith, commitment, and patience. It is not a spectator sport. In fact, it's not a sport at all. It's real life, with eternal life-or-death consequences. We don't say this to scare you but to encourage you to take it seriously. No one can successfully parent alone. We all need God's help.

You might be wondering, *But where do I start?* Let's begin by taking a closer look at the four basic needs we briefly mentioned and how meeting these needs is the practical "how" of godly parenting.

2

Basic Training

To understand the biblical basis for parenting and the skills required to raise children properly, parents must understand the four major needs of a child that only God can completely satisfy. As we mentioned before, these needs are acceptance, identify, security, and purpose.

A child's understanding of who God is and what He is like is most influenced by the character of their parents and their parents' treatment of them. When a parent demonstrates a balance of love and truth and faithfully invests themself in the development of their child, it will be easy for that child to know and love the Lord. But when a parent is absent, rejecting, cruel, or abusive, the child will not have their needs met and will have a more difficult time forming a relationship with God.

> **A child's understanding of who God is and what He is like is most influenced by the character of their parents and their parents' treatment of them.**

Parenting is more caught than taught. In other words, children are much more influenced by who we are and what we do than by what we say or teach. A parent's habits, attitudes, language, friends, church participation, and marriage relationship all have a profound impact on a child. Parents who try to legislate love for God or religious beliefs to their child (beliefs that they themselves are not willing to live out in front of the child) are not parenting properly or providing the role model their child needs.

The twofold purpose of each parent is to:

1. Teach and train a child to know and love God.

2. Meet the four basic needs of the child.

Need #1: Acceptance

A child experiences acceptance by feeling safe and secure wherever they are. Acceptance enhances their sense of self-worth and belonging. When a child experiences rejection rather than acceptance, they feel insecure and detached, and their senses of aloneness and vulnerability are heightened. Consequently, parents must do everything possible to demonstrate love and acceptance to a child from the moment of birth onward. It is important for parents to communicate love and acceptance to their child in four major ways:

1. Physical Affection

When a baby is born, they are often placed directly on the mother's bare chest. This practice is called "skin-to-skin-contact" (or "kangaroo care"), and research shows that there are many benefits to the baby, including:

- better digestion
- better body temperature maintenance
- improved weight gain
- higher blood oxygen levels
- stronger immune systems.

Moms also benefit from skin-to-skin contact. Their oxytocin levels increase, reducing their blood pressure, lowering stress levels, and helping restore pre-pregnancy hormone levels.[1]

Even babies who have to go into the neonatal intensive care unit (NICU) have been shown to benefit from physical touch. Look at these incredible statistics of babies who received standard medical care plus skin-to-skin contact versus babies who only received standard care:

- 36 percent lower death rate

- 50 percent lower risk of sepsis

- 78 percent less likely to develop hypothermia

- 88 percent less likely to have dangerously lower blood sugar[2]

God made us to experience and benefit from physical affection. When parents regularly touch and hold their children in a warm, appropriate fashion, acceptance is communicated to them in a powerful way. And this isn't just for babies. Did you know that your children "crave touch and actually require it for normal physical, social, and emotional development to occur"? In fact, "many systems in the brain are activated by touch, without which optimal physiological development is not possible."[3]

The less parents touch and hold their children, the more emotionally detached and rejected the children are likely to feel. I (Jimmy) had a father who didn't touch me from the time I was three years old until I was 38 years. That's a 35-year gap! My mother wasn't very affectionate either. This lack of physical touch, also called "touch deprivation" or "skin hunger," had a tremendous impact on my life. Research shows that skin hunger increases feelings of loneliness, anxiety, depression. The body increases its production of the stress hormone cortisol, which makes your heart rate, blood pressure, respiration rate, and muscle tension all go up.[4]

When I finally came into puberty and began to experience sexual feelings, I was overwhelmed by the desire to have physical contact with girls. I was trying to fill a void in my mind and my body. Part of this attraction was normal development, of course, but I truly believe my desires would have been less intense if I had been raised with normal physical affection from my parents.

2. Verbal Affirmation

All children need to hear their parents say they love them every day. Yes, every single day. They also need to be praised and complimented throughout their lives. When children grow up in an atmosphere of verbal affirmation, they bond to their parents and grow up believing in themselves. However, if there is an atmosphere of quietness or criticism, children will sense a lack of acceptance.

Unless there is an emergency such as a child running into the street, parents should not yell at their children. It is rejecting and hostile. Parents must never bully or shame their children. Shame is solely a weapon of the enemy, and as parents, we must not use it as a tool for control. Please don't ever tell your children, "I'm ashamed of you." Your child is a person created in the image of God. Now, this doesn't mean you condone, enable, or approve of all their actions. Absolutely not. Your child's choices may be totally unacceptable, but your child is not.

3. Availability

A lot has been said and written about spending *quality* time with children, but children also need large *quantities* of time around their parents, especially when they are younger. Parents who spend too much time at work, at church, with friends, or doing other things leave their children feeling alone and unimportant. (We will talk more about priorities in the "Chain of Command" chapter.)

Children spell love "t-i-m-e." It's hard to believe that I (Julie) have college-age daughters, and Cory and I are empty-nesters! But

there is a sofa at the end of our bed, and when our girls were growing up, they would sit on the sofa and talk with us. The four of us
had all kinds of conversations about life, and our girls knew that
they could talk to us about anything on that sofa.

Children spell love "t-i-m-e."

We all need to live a balanced life with many interests, but we
must protect a healthy amount of time and energy to spend with our
children. This lets them know we accept them and care for them.

4. Expression

There are two things every child needs from parents: a sense
of belonging and a sense of identity and individual expression.
A healthy person always has a balanced sense of who they are
and to whom they belong. An unhealthy person either feels a
lack of belonging or a lack of identity. Therefore, as parents, we
need to let our children know we respect their feelings, opinions,
and individuality. Although we must teach our children to obey
us and conform to certain standards, we must not overwhelm
their individual identities with our own opinions or dominant
personalities.

Parents who try to over-control a child's life or make that child
into something they want them to be are harming the child. Yes,
parents should lead a child in the right direction, but they also
should give the child room to be an individual and to make certain
personal choices.

As a child gets older, their freedom must increase until finally,
one day, that child is on their own, having a sense of personal
identity and a sense of belonging to loving parents.

Need #2: Identity

All of us have a deep need to feel unique and significant. Parents communicate this sense of identity to their children by letting them know how special they are. A child should not be compared to brothers or sisters or made to overly conform to the family system. Rather, a child should be allowed to express themself in an atmosphere of love and order.

I (Jimmy) remember one young man being emotionally crushed by his father, who pushed the son throughout his life to be a football player. When the young man resisted, the father browbeat him and tried to make him feel guilty. Although a parent sometimes needs to make a child do something the parent knows is best, care must be taken to try not to make a child live the parent's personal plan for his life.

The older children get, the more their feelings and opinions should dictate the direction of their lives. Children should not be given the freedom to self-destruct, but they should have the right to be who God made them to be and to find themselves within safe parameters and in His will.

As an example, I (Julie) have an uncle who was the administrator of a psychiatric hospital. One day a man was admitted who was having a breakdown. He had recently graduated from dental school, and as the doctors began to examine him, they realized his problem was relatively simple. All of this man's uncles, brothers, and his dad were dentists, and all of his life he was told that he was going to be a dentist. So without questioning it, he went to dental school. But, on the day he graduated, this man had to face the reality of being a dentist for the rest of his life.

As he said to the psychiatrist treating him, "I hate being a dentist. I hate having my hands in people's mouths. The last thing I want to be is a dentist and I just can't believe that now I am one." His parents were probably very good, well-intentioned people, but they tried to force him into the family model without regard for his unique personal identity.

Need #3: Security

A child's sense of security is derived chiefly from the stability of their parents' lives. Therefore, when a child senses strife in the home, they immediately will feel insecure. Parents need to respect the natural sensitivity and emotional vulnerability of their children. Even if parents know their disagreements are not going to end in divorce, the children do not need to hear them argue. Children need to see their parents love and serve one another.

Children also need patient instruction and communication concerning their fears and things they need to know about life in general. Children feel secure when they are in an atmosphere of stability and love. Parents need to do everything possible to create this type of environment for their children. Setting parameters and disciplining them lovingly and properly also makes them feel secure in the family environment of love.

Children need rules and boundaries, and they need to be held accountable when they disobey and rebel. Children feel loved and secure when they are raised with a balance of accountability and acceptance.

> ## Children feel loved and secure when they are raised with a balance of accountability and acceptance.

Need #4: Purpose

Even when a child is young, they need to be taught that God has a special purpose for their life. As we tell them they are special and unique to us and to God, we need also to let them know that God created them for a special purpose that will be revealed someday.

As parents, we meet our children's need for purpose by giving them responsibilities around the house and with the family. Children need to learn to pick up their toys and keep their rooms clean. As they get older, parents should continue to give them increased duties and responsibilities, but this should be done in a balanced way. Children should be neither houseguests nor servants. They are part of the family, and every member of the family receives respect and responsibility.

Balancing responsibilities with the fun children need requires sensitivity on the part of parents. Children should have time to be children, to play and have fun with friends, yet they should do their part of the chores around the house. This is a critical part of making them feel fulfilled and important.

We also need to encourage children to serve in church and in the community. Children need to be educated from the Bible about their spiritual giftings and how to use these gifts to help and serve others. From the time our children are young, we need to pray for them to find and fulfill their ministries for God.

No person will ever feel fulfilled or have a true purpose in life until they are fulfilling God's call on their life. We will be judged not only for the good and bad things we have done, but also according to whether or not we have obeyed God's will for our lives.

When a child is taught to be productive and responsible, they are happier and feel that they have a purpose. However, when a child is allowed to be irresponsible and lazy or is never taught to obey God's will for their life, they will be unfulfilled and unhappy. Therefore, from the time children are young, parents need to give them responsibilities and instructions appropriate for their age and abilities.

———————

When a child is grown and ready to leave home, the parents should be able to say two things:

1. "We have done everything we could to teach and train our child to know and love God."

2. "We have met every major need in our child's life in a faithful and sacrificial manner."

If a person can truthfully make those two statements, they have been a successful parent. And this is truly commendable because success doesn't come without difficulty. Society has all kinds of opinions about raising children, and we have to be diligent to find out what God's Word says and then follow it. And as we pursue God the way He commands—loving Him with all our soul—and teach our children to do the same, there is an enemy who tries to stop us. We must understand who this enemy is and what his schemes are in order to defeat him.

3

THE Soul War

What is a *soul*? You have probably heard this word used in a variety of ways. When someone dies, people often say, "God rest her soul." Someone sharing their deepest feelings is thought to be "baring his soul." When pilots count the people on their flights, they refer to the number of "souls onboard." And, of course, there is an entire genre of music called "soul music." Soul is a common word, but do people really know what it means? And why would there ever be a war over it?

The Soul

The concept of *soul* (from the Old English *sāwol*) can be found all the way back in Genesis. On the sixth day of creation, "the LORD God formed man of the dust of the ground, and breathed into his nostrils the breath of life; and man became a living **soul**" (Genesis 2:7 KJV, bold added). Now, Genesis was written in Hebrew, and the Hebrew word for soul is *nephesh* (pronounced neh'-fesh). Man was just a dust-made body at first, but with God's breath, he became a *nephesh*. According to Strong's Concordance, *nephesh* can be defined as "living being, life, self, person" but also "desire, passion, appetite, [and] emotion."[1] Keep all those words in mind as you read these verses with *nephesh*:

21

He makes me to lie down in green pastures;
He leads me beside the still waters.
He restores my soul [*nephesh*] (Psalm 23:2–3).

My soul [*nephesh*] longs, yes, even faints
For the courts of the LORD;
My heart and my flesh cry out for the living God (Psalm 84:2.)

I will greatly rejoice in the LORD,
My soul [*nephesh*] shall be joyful in my God;
For He has clothed me with the garments of salvation (Isaiah 61:10).

Nephesh appears 754 times in the Old Testament, and it is often used to describe a person's essence—the very fiber of their being. The restoration of your soul is the restoration of your very self. To long for the Lord's courts is to long with all your passion. And to be joyful in God is to rejoice with all your emotion.

Let's look at the New Testament now, which was written in Greek. The Greek equivalent of *nephesh* is *psuché* (pronounced psoo-khay'). It literally means 'breath' and is used to denote "the vital force," "that in which there is life," and "the seat of the feelings, desires, affections, [and] aversions."[2] *Psuché* can also be transliterated as *psyche*, and this is the root of our English word psychology (literally "the study of the soul").

Here are some New Testament verses with *psuché*:

Take My yoke upon you and learn from Me, for I am gentle and lowly in heart, and you will find rest for your souls [*psuché*] (Matthew 11:29).

For what will it profit a man if he gains the whole world, and loses his own soul [*psuché*]? (Mark 8:36).

So get rid of all the filth and evil in your lives, and humbly accept the word God has planted in your hearts, for it has the power to save your souls [*psuché*] (James 1:21 NLT).

Soul-rest is rest in the deepest part of you. If you lose your soul, you lose everything, but God's Word has the power to save your very being.

In the first chapter, we examined two Scriptures that outline our purpose as humans. Let's look at those again, this time in light of the full meaning of *nephesh* and *psuché*:

> Hear, O Israel: The LORD our God, the LORD is one! You shall love the LORD your God with all your heart, with all your soul [*nephesh*], and with all your strength (Deuteronomy 6:4).

> Jesus replied, "The most important commandment is this: 'Listen, O Israel! The LORD our God is the one and only LORD. And you must love the LORD your God with all your heart, all your soul [*psuché*], all your mind, and all your strength'" (Mark 12:29–30 NLT).

Loving the Lord with all your *nephesh* and *psuché* means loving Him with everything you have and holding nothing back. You cannot deny Him any portion of your being. Every part of your self—your desires, passions, appetites, emotions, feelings, affections, etc.—is completely surrendered. This is what God requires. This is how we fulfill our purpose as humans to know and love Him. And this is the ultimate goal toward which we teach and train our children.

> **Loving the Lord with all your *nephesh* and *psuché* means loving Him with everything you have and holding nothing back.**

The Enemy

When you surrender your soul to the Lord, you position yourself to accomplish His perfect plan for your life. Nothing has the power to stop you. It's incredible! But that doesn't mean it will always be easy. You see, you have you an enemy—Satan—who has one mission: "to steal and kill and destroy" (John 10:10 NLT). He will do anything and everything to try to stop people from living for God, and this includes declaring war not only on your soul but also on the soul of your child.

As believers, we need to understand three things. First, Satan is our enemy because we stand with Jesus. Satan wasn't our enemy when we were living in darkness, sin, and deception. Back then, we weren't opposing him, so he had no reason to oppose us. But the nature of salvation is acknowledging the truth of who Jesus is and putting our faith in Him. In John 14:6, Jesus said, "I am the way, the truth, and the life." Satan, on the other hand, hates the truth—"He was a murderer from the beginning, not holding to the truth, for there is no truth in him. When he lies, he speaks his native language, for he is a liar and the father of lies" (John 8:44 NIV). When we surrender to Jesus, Satan's power over us is broken, and we are no longer in bondage to sin, lies, and death. We are free! And when this happens, the enemy's war against us begins.

The second thing believers need to know is this: Satan cannot take away our salvation, but he can take away our joy and victory if we don't understand his nature and how he attacks us. First Peter 4:8 says, "Be sober, be vigilant; because your adversary the devil walks about like a roaring lion, seeking whom he may devour." Why does the enemy seem to devour some people but not others? It's not a matter of being saved or unsaved; rather, it's a matter of being protected or unprotected. Faith in Jesus Christ saves us, but faith in God's Word protects us. The Bible is not merely a how-to manual for good living. No, it's our foundation, our weapon, and our light.

Therefore whoever hears these sayings of Mine, and does them, I will liken him to a wise man who built his house on the rock: and the rain descended, the floods came, and the winds blew and beat on that house; and it did not fall, for it was founded on the rock.

> But everyone who hears these sayings of Mine, and does not do them, will be like a foolish man who built his house on the sand: and the rain descended, the floods came, and the winds blew and beat on that house; and it fell. And great was its fall (Matthew 7:24–27).

A foundation protects a house against inevitable storms. Jesus promises us victory if we will make the Word of God the foundation of our lives. So many well-meaning Christian families are being devoured today because parents are not using the Bible as the foundation for the way they raise their children. It's not wrong to want your children to be popular, well-educated, or successful in their career, but did you know that they can be all those things and still be miserable? On the other hand, Psalm 1:1–3 gives this promise:

> Oh, the joys of those who do not
>> follow the advice of the wicked,
>> or stand around with sinners,
>> or join in with mockers.
> But they delight in the law of the LORD,
>> meditating on it day and night.
> They are like trees planted along the riverbank,
>> bearing fruit each season.
> Their leaves never wither,
>> and they prosper in all they do (NLT).

Did you catch that final line? "They prosper in all they do" (v. 3). This prosperity isn't based on legalism. When people meet me (Julie) and learn that my parents are Jimmy and Karen Evans, they often assume I grew up with family devotions every single night. But that wasn't the case in our home because my parents realized that *every* moment is a teachable moment. They used regular, daily occurrences like driving somewhere in the car or eating dinner together to infuse the truth of God's Word in our lives.

In listing the armor of God in Ephesians chapter 6, the apostle Paul calls the Word of God "the sword of the Spirit" (v. 17). The sword is the only offensive weapon mentioned, and it's the only one we need. Three times, Satan tried to tempt Jesus in the wilderness, and three times Jesus defeated him by saying, "It is written" and quoting Scripture (see Matthew chapter 4 and Luke chapter 4).

A little child who quotes the Bible is as powerful as any preacher on earth. The power doesn't come from age or experience; it comes from God's Word. Hebrews 4:12 says, "For the word of God is living and powerful, and sharper than any two-edged sword, piercing even to the division of soul and spirit, and of joints and marrow, and is a discerner of the thoughts and intents of the heart." The Word of God is more powerful than any weapon the enemy could ever try to use against us. It is nuclear in the spiritual realm, and it provides total protection.

A little child who quotes the Bible is as powerful as any preacher on earth.

God's Word is our light in darkness. Psalm 119:105 says, "Your word is a lamp to my feet and a light to my path." When we walk in the light of God's Word, we can see and avoid the traps Satan has laid out for us. Most believers accept that God has a plan for their lives, but we need to realize that the enemy has a plan too. If we try to walk without the light of the Word, we are vulnerable and easily deceived. Satan's first words to a human were, "Has God surely said … ?" The enemy wants to plant doubts in our minds about God's Word because in order to defeat us, he has to first disarm us. For the sake of our souls and the souls of our children, we must remain squarely under the light of God's Word.

When Karen and I (Jimmy) were in our mid-20s, we moved into a new-to-us house. God had saved our marriage from the brink of divorce, but we started fighting again. I can't even remember the reason now, but for about a week, we were on each other's nerves. On the night that we usually went to our discipleship group, Karen came up to me while I was watching football on TV and said, "Hey, it's time to go to our discipleship group." I said, "I'm not going." She tried to get me to go, but I refused, and my reason was simple: I knew it would bother her. So Karen went to the discipleship group by herself.

A few hours later, she came home and sat down right in front of me. Very seriously, she said, "I need to tell you something." I thought, *Oh, good, she's going to repent!* But what Karen actually said was this: "Sarah (the lead of the group) was praying for us this week, and she saw a lion's head in our living room. It was roaring at us and trying to break us up. We need to hold hands, pray, and take authority over the devil." We had never done that before. (I thought people who did that were weird!) But as soon as Karen said it, I knew she was right, and for the first time, we held hands and prayed together. We said, "In the name of Jesus, we bind you, Satan. We take authority over you and command you to leave." The instant we prayed, it was like someone sprayed Lysol in our house and opened the drapes. The entire atmosphere of our home changed, and I looked at Karen and wondered, *Now, why was I mad at you?* I honestly couldn't remember.

The third thing believers need to know is that we can protect ourselves and our families against Satan. Your children do *not* have to fall prey to the enemy's schemes. The way we do this is total commitment to the Word of God.

For the mystery of lawlessness is already at work; only He who now restrains will do so until He is taken out of the way. And then the lawless one will be revealed, whom the Lord will consume with the breath of His mouth and destroy with the brightness of His coming. The coming of the lawless one is according to the working of Satan, with all power, signs, and lying wonders, and with all unrighteous deception among those who perish, because they did not receive **the love of the truth**, that they might be saved. And for this reason God will send them strong delusion, that they should believe the lie, that they all may be condemned who did not believe the truth but had pleasure in unrighteousness (2 Thessalonians 2:7–12, bold added).

The Greek word for love in this passage is *agape*, and it means total commitment regardless of how you feel or the circumstances. Jesus said, "For whoever is ashamed of Me and My words in this adulterous and sinful generation, of him the Son of Man also will be ashamed when He comes in the glory of His Father with the holy angels" (Mark 8:38). There is no halfway commitment to God's Word. We either believe it, or we don't. We either take it seriously, or we don't. If we want the promises of God's Word for ourselves and our children, then we must base our lives on it. And if we do, then we will easily overcome the enemy.

Now, being committed to God's Word doesn't mean we are perfect. We will never be perfect as long as we are on this earth. Satan knows that, and if he can't take the Word from us, then he will try to use it against us to condemn us. When he does this, we have to use the Word against him as our foundation, our sword, and our light. Remember, we are saved by the grace of God, not by works. Here are two passages we can stand on:

But God, who is rich in mercy, because of His great love with which He loved us, even when we were dead in trespasses, made us alive together with Christ (by grace you have been saved), and raised us up together, and made us sit together in the heavenly places in Christ Jesus, that in the ages to come He might show the exceeding riches of His grace in His kindness toward us in Christ Jesus. For by grace you have been saved through faith, and that not of yourselves; it is the gift of God, not of works, lest anyone should boast (Ephesians 2:4–9).

So now there is no condemnation for those who belong to Christ Jesus. And because you belong to him, the power of the life-giving

Spirit has freed you from the power of sin that leads to death (Romans 8:1–2 NLT).

Parents, if you are a follower of Jesus Christ, you have a real enemy waging real warfare against your family. Satan would love to stop this next generation from growing "in the grace and knowledge of our Lord and Savior Jesus Christ" (2 Peter 3:18), and if he gets the chance to devour your child's soul, he's going to take it.

You might be thinking, *That sounds awfully intense. I don't want to fight anyone; I just want to live in peace.* However, in this fallen world, peace only comes *after* victory, and victory only comes after the fight.

The God of the universe chose *you* to be your child's parent. It doesn't matter if they came to you via sex, adoption, foster care, or some other method. You are a parent, and you have a God-given duty to fight for your child.

The God of the universe chose *you* to be your child's parent.

Are you ready? Good, because it's time to stand up and get dressed.

4

Dressed To Kill

No one wants to go to war in their underwear. Nor should they. Aside from looking ridiculous, they would be exposed with zero protection. The enemy would quickly spot the easy target and finish them off before the battle had even begun.

You may not be able to see Satan, but the war for the soul is still a war, and like any military conflict, it requires armor.

Finally, be strong in the Lord and in the strength of His might. Put on the full armor of God, so that you will be able to stand firm against the schemes of the devil. For our struggle is not against flesh and blood, but against the rulers, against the powers, against the world forces of this darkness, against the spiritual *forces* of wickedness in the heavenly *places*. Therefore, take up the full armor of God, so that you will be able to resist on the evil day, and having done everything, to stand firm. Stand firm therefore, having belted your waist with truth, and having put on the breastplate of righteousness, and having strapped on your feet the preparation of the gospel of peace; in addition to all, taking up the shield of faith with which you will be able to extinguish all the flaming arrows of the evil *one*. And take the helmet of salvation and the sword of the Spirit, which is the word of God (Ephesians 6:10–18 NASB).

To summarize, here are the pieces of the armor of God:

- Belt of truth

- Breastplate of righteousness

- Shoes of the gospel of peace

- Shield of faith

- Helmet of salvation

- Sword of the Spirit.

Now, if we could offer you a spiritual mirror, what would you see in the reflection? Would you be covered head to toe, or would you be in your underwear? People tend to treat the armor of God like an à la carte menu. "Oh, I think I'll choose the shoes of peace today." "Oh, the shield of faith sounds nice." They fail to realize that the armor of God is a fixed menu. It's all or nothing. A friend of ours made this clever observation: "If the armor of God was clothing, it would be a onesie." You're either covered head to toe, or you're in your underwear. There's no in-between. That's why Paul says, "Put on the **full** armor of God" (bold added).

Sometimes the enemy will try to sneak past you, and other times he will come at you with a head-on attack. As we will explain throughout this book, Satan has no legitimate authority or power over your family, but that doesn't stop him from trying. One pastor aptly explains it this way: "Though Satan has been decisively defeated, and his future is doomed, he lives for the present. He still schemes (2 Corinthians 2:11), stalks (1 Peter 5:8), deceives (Revelation 12:9), ensnares (2 Timothy 2:26), hinders (1 Thessalonians 2:18), harasses (2 Corinthians 12:7), and attacks us with fiery darts of temptation (Ephesians 6:16)."[1]

Let's look at all the parts of the armor of God so that we can better understand how we can withstand the attacks of the enemy:

Belt of Truth

Having belted your waist with truth (v.14).

Today, belts aren't very special. They serve the basic function of holding up our pants and not much else. However, when the apostle Paul wrote about the amor of God, the belt was the central piece of a Roman soldier's armor. It was called the *cingulum*, and it served the practical purpose of carrying the scabbard (the sheath) that held the soldier's sword. The *cingulum* had leather strips (*baltea*) hanging down to protect the lower part of the soldier's body, and it also connected to the breastplate. Without his *cingulum*, a soldier was unprepared and ill-equipped for battle. In fact, you might say that a soldier without a *cingulum* wasn't really a soldier at all.

The same is accurate for believers and truth. Truth not only protects and defends us, but it also defines us. The word Paul uses for truth is *aléthia*. It means 'reality,' 'sincerity,' and 'divine truth revealed to man,'[2] and it's the same word Jesus uses to describe Himself when He says that He is the truth (see John 14:6).

Truth not only protects and defends us, but it also defines us.

Have you ever heard the phrase, "I'm just living my truth"? Society wants you to believe that truth is relative, that it changes based on a person's understanding or opinion. Of course, this goes against the very definition of truth, which is "being in accord with fact or reality."[3] Facts don't change just because you disagree with them; reality doesn't shift because you don't like it. Hebrews 13:8 says, "Jesus Christ *is* the same yesterday, today, and forever." Truth is based solely on Him, and because He doesn't change, it doesn't change either.

If someone asked us how to get to Dallas, Texas, they would probably be confused to hear, "Oh, just take whatever highway you want. All roads lead to Dallas." That would be silly because all roads do *not* lead to Dallas. The same is true for faith and salvation. All faiths do *not* lead to salvation. There is one way to salvation, and His name is Jesus Christ.

Breastplate of Righteousness

Having put on the breastplate of righteousness (v. 14).

A Roman soldier's breastplate was made of metal bands that overlapped and were tied together with leather cords. It was light and flexible enough to be worn while running, and it covered the soldier from chest to hips. Without a breastplate, a soldier's vital organs, such as his heart, lungs, and digestive tract, were exposed, and he could easily be taken out by the enemy.

As believers, we need to understand that our hearts are not naturally good. Jeremiah 17:9 says, "The heart is deceitful above all *things*, and desperately wicked." And Jesus Himself said, "For out of the heart proceed evil thoughts, murders, adulteries, fornications, thefts, false witness, blasphemies" (Matthew 15:19). This is why we so desperately need righteousness.

Righteousness is being right with God, which happens through faith. Paul writes in Romans 3:22, "We are made right with God by placing our faith in Jesus Christ. And this is true for everyone who believes, no matter who we are" (NLT). You can't have righteousness without truth because you can't be right with God without Jesus. He is "the Lord our righteousness" (Jeremiah 23:6 NASB).

Shoes of the Gospel of Peace

Having strapped on your feet the preparation of the gospel of peace (v. 15).

Roman soldiers wore battle shoes called *caligae*. *Caligae* were sandals made of leather strips attached to a sole that had studs (or spikes) across the bottom. The leather strips were strategically placed not to create blisters, even on long marches, and the studs served the dual purposes of protecting feet from difficult terrain and attacking enemies that had fallen on the ground.

Paul says that we are to put the "gospel of peace" on our feet. In other words, the gospel of peace serves as our spiritual battle shoes. The word "gospel" comes from the Greek *euaggelion*, which means 'good news,' and it always points to Jesus, our Prince of Peace (Isaiah 40:1). In Romans 5:1–2, Paul writes, "Therefore, since we have been justified through faith, we have peace with God through our Lord Jesus Christ, through whom we have gained access by faith into this grace in which we now stand" (NIV).

After meeting Jesus on the road to Damascus, Paul walked countless miles to share the good news of Jesus Christ all over his part of the world. He faced severe persecution from Jews and Gentiles alike, but he never gave up, even to the point of death. Today, we have access to incredible advancements in transportation and communication methods, but we still have the same mission. We must prepare our feet with the gospel of peace and march forward, always keeping Paul's words in the forefront of our minds:

> How then shall they call on Him in whom they have not believed? And how shall they believe in Him of whom they have not heard? And how shall they hear without a preacher? And how shall they preach unless they are sent? As it is written:
> "How beautiful are the feet of those who preach the gospel of peace, Who bring glad tidings of good things!" (Romans 10:14–15).

As believers, one of the primary purposes of our lives is to share the gospel, and as parents, we have a special purpose to share it with our children. The basic failure of so much parenting today is the tunnel vision of *me* and *now*, especially regarding money, popularity, power, etc. When the gospel is our purpose, it grounds us, like how shoes with cleats ground athletes to the field. But the gospel gives an eyes-wide-open perspective and an eternal reason for life.

Shield of Faith

> Taking up the shield of faith with which you will be able to extinguish all the flaming arrows of the evil one (v. 16).

A Roman soldier chose his shield by what kind of battle he might face. For riding on horseback or fighting hand to hand, he would carry a round shield called a *parma*, which was about three feet in diameter. The other option was the much larger *scutum*, a curved rectangular shield that was about four feet tall, two and a half feet wide, and more than 20 pounds in weight. It is this second type of shield Paul refers to in the armor of God. The apostle uses the Greek word *thureos*, and readers of his letter would have recognized it as the large, door-shaped shield that could defend not only an individual soldier but also his unit when used together with other such shields.

If faith is our shield, then it's important to understand what faith is. Hebrews 11:1 says, "Now faith is confidence in what we hope for and assurance about what we do not see" (NIV). Verse 6 continues, "And without faith it is impossible to please God, because anyone who comes to him must believe that he exists and that he rewards those who earnestly seek him." We love what one Bible study commentary says about faith:

> You don't hope for what you already have. Faith involves a huge element of trust. We must examine the evidence and see that God has proved Himself to be unchanging and consistent, and then we must firmly believe that He will fulfill His promises to us.[4]

Paul explains, "Faith comes by hearing, and hearing by the word of God" (Romans 10:17). Another translation puts it this way: "Faith

comes from hearing, that is, hearing the Good News about Christ"
(NLT). This hearing is not the in-one-ear-and-out-the-other type.
No, it's sincerely believing that Jesus is who He claimed to be and
that God will do what He said He would do. Faith is like a muscle,
and it grows every time you read the Bible. The basis of our faith is
not our emotions, because those will come and go, but rather the
unwavering, ever-consistent faithfulness of God.

Faith is like a muscle, and it grows every time you read the Bible.

The "flaming arrows of the evil one" can include fear, worry,
discouragement, rejection, doubt, shame, etc. Satan wants to
destroy you by attacking your confidence in God's faithfulness,
but when you raise up your shield of faith, you remind yourself
that "God, who began the good work within you, will continue
his work until it is finally finished on the day when Christ Jesus
returns" (Philippians 1:6 NLT).

Helmet of Salvation

Take the helmet of salvation (v. 17).

A Roman soldier's helmet was called a *galea*, and it served both to
protect his head and to identify him as a particular rank.

The helmets usually came with cheek guards and were thicker in
places most likely to be hit. Helmets worn by legionaries and centurions had crests made of plumes of horse hair which were usually
dyed red. With the distinct nature of their helmets, it was easy to
identify these men in the midst of a battle. Some ancient historians
such as Polybius assert that the helmet worn by the Roman soldiers
had a psychological function to it. He said in his book *The Histories*

of Polybius that the helmets were adorned with a "circle of feathers" which served to make a soldier appear twice as tall as he actually was.[5]

Roman soldiers understood the importance of their helmets on the battlefield—they knew that a single blow to the head could take them out if they weren't protected. As believers, we need to understand that our minds are the biggest battlefield of our lives. One author explains it this way: "When the enemy attacks, he usually attacks there because he knows if he can influence the way you think, he will influence the way you will act."[6]

When Paul writes about salvation in Ephesians 6:17, he is not referring solely to a person's initial moment of surrendering to Christ and being born again. (We will talk more about that in the next chapter). That is a one-time event, after which we must choose to "take" the helmet of salvation and remind ourselves continually of the incredible hope we have in our Savior. Paul connects salvation and hope in 1 Thessalonians chapter 5:

> But since we belong to the day, let us be sober, putting on faith and love as a breastplate, and **the hope of salvation as a helmet**. For God did not appoint us to suffer wrath but to receive salvation through our Lord Jesus Christ. He died for us so that, whether we are awake or asleep, we may live together with him (vv. 8–10 NIV, bold added).

By taking the helmet of salvation, we declare our allegiance to Jesus and our faith that His perfect work on the cross will result in eternal life. He is our hope! The apostle Peter wrote, "Blessed *be* the God and Father of our Lord Jesus Christ, who according to His abundant mercy has begotten us again to a living hope through the resurrection of Jesus Christ from the dead, to an inheritance incorruptible and undefiled and that does not fade away, reserved in heaven for you" (1 Peter 1:3–4).

The Sword of the Spirit

We have briefly mentioned the sword of the Spirit (the Word of God), which is the only offensive weapon listed in Ephesians chapter 6. While many people might think of the long, heavy weapon wielded by medieval knights, the Greek word Paul uses is *machaira*. A *machaira* was "a short sword or dagger,"[7] about 18–22 inches long, designed to be used in hand-to-hand combat. It had an extremely sharp blade and a curved tip that could not only stab an enemy but also remove his entrails when twisted and removed. No one wanted to mess with a *machaira!*

The Word of God is our *machaira* against the enemy. It lights our path (Psalm 119:105), defeats temptation (Matthew 4:1–11), removes condemnation (Romans 8:1), and guarantees salvation (John 3:16; Hebrews 7:25). We use it to "demolish strongholds ... [and] arguments and every pretension that sets itself up against the knowledge of God, and we take captive every thought to make it obedient to Christ" (2 Corinthians 10:4–5 NIV). The Word of God absolutely decimates the enemy, which is why Satan tries everything he can to prevent believers from understanding its power.

Every piece of the armor of God points to Jesus Christ. He is our truth, our righteousness, and our peace. We put our faith in Him, our salvation comes from Him, and His word defeats the enemy.

Here's a story from Scripture you may not have heard before that explains how going into battle without Jesus is never a good idea:

> Some of the Jewish exorcists, who went from place to place, attempted to use the name of the Lord Jesus over those who had the evil spirits, saying, "I order you in the name of Jesus whom Paul preaches!" Now there were seven sons of Sceva, a Jewish chief priest, doing this. But the evil spirit responded and said to them, "I recognize Jesus, and I know of Paul, but who are you?" And the man in whom was

the evil spirit, pounced on them and subdued all of them and over-powered them, so that they fled out of that house naked and wounded (Acts 19:13–16 NASB).

The sons of Sceva tried to use the name of Jesus because they recognized that it was a powerful weapon. But they had no relationship with Jesus and, therefore, no authority to use His name. They charged into battle and came out naked—literally.

You can't trick Satan into thinking you're wearing the armor of God. He's a better liar than you are. We looked at this verse before, but let's read it one more time: "He was a murderer from the beginning, not holding to the truth, for there is no truth in him. When he lies, he speaks his native language, for he is a liar and the father of lies" (John 8:44 NIV). Because Satan is the "father of lies," he has no trouble spotting another liar. The only way to make him think you're wearing the armor of God is for you to actually wear the armor of God. And the only way to wear the armor of God is to have a relationship with Jesus Christ.

You can't trick Satan into thinking you're wearing the armor of God.

5

Weapons Check

Are you prepared to step onto the battlefield and fight for your children? It may be a bit intimidating, but if you know Jesus as your Lord and Savior, then the answer is yes. However, if you have not surrendered your life to Jesus, then you have a very important decision to make, one that will affect not only your parenting skills but also every other area of your life.

What Does It Mean to Be Born Again?

In John 3:7, Jesus tells Nicodemus, "You must be born again" (NIV). To understand this phrase, we need to take a quick trip back to the Garden of Eden. After God created Adam and Eve as livings souls and placed them in the garden, He warned them not to eat of the fruit of the tree of the knowledge of good and evil. The reason was clear: if they ate it, they would die (see Genesis 2:17).

Genesis chapter 3 records how Satan, in the form of a serpent, tempted Adam and Eve, and they ate the forbidden fruit. The moment they ate it, the Spirit of God departed from them, and they became spiritually dead. They could no longer commune with God intimately, as they had done when He walked with them in the garden.

They were now separated from God, and as a result, their souls became darkened and corrupted, their relationship divided, and their bodies aged and decayed. They passed their fallen nature on to their children and the generations after them until the entire human race became utterly evil (see Genesis 6:5–6).

To this day, spiritual death and the natural tendency to rebel against God are inherent in every person. Sin is a sickness that infects everyone. Thankfully, there is a cure.

> For God so loved the world that He gave His only begotten Son, that whoever believes in Him should not perish but have everlasting life. For God did not send His Son into the world to condemn the world, but that the world through Him might be saved (John 3:16–17).

Jesus, the Son of God, came to earth, lived a sinless life, and died the most painful death imaginable on the cross in order to pay for the sins of all mankind. Then, three days later, He rose again, having defeated the power of sin and death once and for all.

Being "born again" (also called being "saved") is a free gift you receive instantly when you open your heart to Jesus and accept Him as your Lord and Savior. He will forgive all your sins, allowing you to have the relationship with God you were created to enjoy. He will give you the gift of eternal life in heaven, and He will take you with Him when He comes back to gather His people. God does all this because of His great love for you. Instead of being dead in your sin, you can have new life with Jesus.

So how do you receive salvation? Romans 10:9–10 makes it simple: "If you declare with your mouth, 'Jesus is Lord,' and believe in your heart that God raised him from the dead, you will be saved. For it is with your heart that you believe and are justified, and it is with your mouth that you profess your faith and are saved" (NIV). There are two crucial issues to understand in becoming a true believer in Christ. First, without acknowledging the lordship of Christ, we are simply buying "fire insurance" to save us from hell and make us feel better. A profession of faith that doesn't acknowledge Christ as Lord doesn't change the fundamental problem between God and us—rebellion (see Matthew 7:22–23). Also, believing that God raised Jesus from the dead is essential because it signifies that only Jesus, and no other so-called savior, guru, or religious leader, satisfied the requirements of God to save us from our sins. The resurrection was God's public and eternal validation that Jesus was who He said He was and that His sacrifice for our sins was accepted.

A profession of faith that doesn't acknowledge Christ as Lord doesn't change the fundamental problem between God and us—rebellion.

Salvation occurs as we believe and confess in accordance with God's will. That is all we have to do. Jesus did the hard part for us that we never could have done. Now, by believing and confessing, we can freely receive salvation from God. There is nothing we can do to deserve it. We can only accept it or reject it.

When I (Jimmy) was growing up, my family attended church regularly, and I considered myself to be Christian. But my life was an immoral and rebellious mess. By the time I graduated from high school and went to college, I was completely absorbed in living to please myself and gratifying every desire I had, regardless of what anyone else thought about it. If there was an award for "best at sinning," I definitely would have been a top contender.

Karen and I had started dating when we were in sophomores in high school, and she accepted Christ around that same time. I liked how pure she was, but I didn't share her passion for the Lord. In fact, as she grew her in faith, I became worse and worse. Our dating relationship was very rocky, and Karen broke up with me multiple times. Still, when I proposed during my second year of college, she said yes. I thought everything was going to be great—I could have Karen *and* my ungodly friends and unrighteous behavior. (At that point she didn't know how immoral I was.)

One week before our wedding, everything came crashing down. At my bachelor party, I got drunk and cheated on Karen. Now, I had been drunk and immoral many nights before, and I had never felt guilty about it. But the morning after cheating on Karen, I looked at myself in the bathroom mirror, and for the first time, I didn't like the person staring back at me. I knew I had sinned against Karen and, more importantly, against God. And even though I had never paid much attention in church, I remembered our preacher's words: "If Jesus isn't Lord of all, He isn't Lord at all." Karen didn't know who I really was, but God did.

Standing in the bathroom, I realized I didn't want to live this way any longer. I prayed, "Lord Jesus, I am so sorry for my sin and rebellion. Today I make You the Lord of my life and surrender everything to You. I will live the rest of my life for You and not turn back. This isn't about Karen. I know she may not marry me because of what I have done. Regardless, I will follow You from now on. Please forgive me of my sins and come into my heart and be my Lord and Savior."

That prayer radically changed my life. I knew the first thing I had to do was confess what I had to done to Karen, and when I did, she refused to marry me. Even though I was heartbroken, I kept my commitment to the Lord. He told me never to see my friends again, so I broke off all those relationships that very day. I was very much alone—just me and Jesus. The next day, I called Karen and asked if we could talk. I went to her house, and when she opened the door, I was crying. I came in and sat on her couch and just sobbed. I told Karen how sorry I was and that I completely understood why she didn't want to marry me.

I (Karen) could see that Jimmy's brokenness and repentance was real. In the four years we had dated, he had never apologized once for anything. This was a totally new Jimmy! Not only was I able to forgive him, but we reconciled, and in 2023, we celebrated our 50th wedding anniversary.

Going to church and being a "good person" doesn't make you a Christian. Being raised by Christian parents or having Christian friends doesn't make you a Christian either. My pastor used to say, "Being in church doesn't make you a Christian any more than standing in a garage makes you a car." You must make a personal decision to open your heart to Christ and invite Him to be your Lord and Savior. It is the most important decision you will ever make, and it won't just change your life—it will change your eternity.

Are you ready to invite Jesus to be your Lord and Savior? If so, pray this prayer:

Father God, I confess that I have sinned against You, and I repent. I believe that You sent Your Son, Jesus, to pay the price for my sins and to restore my relationship with You. Jesus, I accept you as my Lord and Savior. I submit my life to You, and from this day forward I will live to serve You. I believe You have come into my heart and have forgiven me of my sins. I believe I am now saved by your grace. I have the gift of eternal life, and I am now ready for your return. Jesus, I pray You will fill me with Your Holy Spirit and give me the power to change, know You, and live my life for You. Amen!

If you sincerely prayed that prayer, then congratulations! You can be sure that God heard you, and Jesus is now the Lord and Savior of your life. You are eternally changed, and your salvation is secure in Christ. Your name has been written in the book of life in heaven (see Philippians 4:3; Revelation 21:27).

How Can I Be Sure?

It is common for Satan to try to tell you that what you just prayed isn't real or that you are too bad to be forgiven. Don't worry—this happens to almost everyone. He has tried that lie with all three of us at different times in our lives. Every time you hear a voice inside your mind or heart that is trying to discourage you, condemn you, or keep you from getting closer to God or doing God's will, that is the enemy.

All relationships require time, effort, and energy as you learn about each other and develop a deep, loving commitment. The same is true with your relationship with the Lord. Here are seven ways you can know that you are a true believer in Jesus:

1. Confession

If you confess with your mouth the Lord Jesus and believe in your heart that God has raised Him from the dead, you will be saved. For with the heart one believes unto righteousness, and with the mouth confession is made unto salvation (Romans 10:9–10).

You openly declare that Jesus is the Lord of your life, and you surrender His authority.

2. Belief

I am the way, the truth, and the life. No one comes to the Father except through Me (John 14:6).

You believe that Jesus is the only way to salvation—the only way to God the Father.

3. Change

Therefore, if anyone *is* in Christ, *he is* a new creation; old things have passed away; behold, all things have become new (2 Corinthians 5:17).

The life of a true believer will change after accepting Christ. This doesn't mean you're perfect. It just means you're somehow different.

4. Hearing

My sheep hear My voice, and I know them, and they follow Me. And I give them eternal life, and they shall never perish; neither shall anyone snatch them out of My hand (John 10:27–28).

God speaks your language. He doesn't necessarily speak to you the same way He speaks to another person, but if you're a Christian, there should be some sense of God's voice and presence in your life.

5. *Grace*

For by grace you have been saved through faith, and that not of your-selves; it is the gift of God, not of works, lest anyone should boast (Ephesians 2:8).

Christians believe they are saved by grace and not by works—not by being a good person or trying to earn their way to heaven.

6. *God's Word*

If you abide in My word, you are My disciples indeed. And you shall know the truth, and the truth shall make you free (John 8:31–32).

In John chapter 1 and Revelation chapter 19, Jesus is called the Word of God. If you don't have a relationship with the Word, then you don't have a relationship with Jesus. If the truth of the Bible turns you off or embarrasses you, that's a major warning sign.

7. *Love*

A new commandment I give to you, that you love one another; as I have loved you, that you also love one another. By this all will know that you are My disciples, if you have love for one another (John 13:34–35).

Some people are hard to love, even within the Church. God loves them, but as humans it can be hard to have patience and grace. We're all imperfect people. But if you're a true Christian, you love God's family. You have a concern and a compassion for fellow believers.

I (Jimmy) wrote a book called *Ten Steps Toward Christ*, and it is all about discovering who God is, what His Word says, and how you can grow stronger in your faith every day. The more you grow into your relationship with God, the more you will learn how to discern the truth from the enemy's lies.

Why Does It Matter?

Why did we bring salvation into a book on parenting? Are the two even related? *Absolutely.* Surrendering own your life to God is the essential first step to fighting for your child's soul.

Are we saying you can't be a good parent if you aren't a Christian? Not at all. There are billions of non-Christian parents all over the world who love their kids and do their very best to protect and provide for them and raise up them to be decent people. But fighting for the soul of your child isn't about being a good parent raising a good kid. It's about being a *godly* parent raising a *godly* kid. You can't be godly without God. People try all the time, and some do a fairly good job of faking it. But it isn't real. It's a façade that's going to come crashing down.

You can't be godly without God.

Here's a truth every parent needs to take to heart: your children won't be more spiritual than you. From the day they are born until the day they leave your home, your children are guided by everything you do and say. The old phrase "Do as I say, not as I do" is a logical fallacy when it comes to parenting. You might be able to force your child to do what you say while they are young and dependent on you for their every need, but as soon as they realize that you don't "do" it yourself, the countdown to rebellion is on. Your life will always speak louder than your lips.

Satan doesn't want your child to know and love God, and he is going to fight against you every step of the way. In the war for your child's soul, the only way to defeat the enemy is to "put on the full armor of God, so that you will be able to stand firm against the schemes of the devil" (Ephesians 6:11 NASB). By surrendering your life to Jesus Christ, you gain full access to this armor. You are no longer standing on the battlefield in your underwear. You are a warrior, and you are ready for whatever the enemy might use to bring you down, including one of his most sinister weapons. We'll talk about that next.

6

Missile Launch

There are plenty of weapons the enemy uses against godly parents, but in this chapter, we're going to focus on one that is particularly devious. It's subtle, it's crafty, and it's the demonic version of a torpedo in a person's life that's guaranteed to sink you the moment you enter the battlefield.

The weapon we're talking about is unforgiveness. Now, before you roll your eyes and dismiss us as overreacting, "holier-than-thou Christians," we aren't asking you to take our word for it. We're going to examine God's Word to see what He says about unforgiveness and then discuss how this applies practically to your life. You just might be surprised.

Unforgiveness

Then Peter came to Him [Jesus] and said, "Lord, how often shall my brother sin against me, and I forgive him? Up to seven times?"

Jesus said to him, "I do not say to you, up to seven times, but up to seventy times seven. Therefore the kingdom of heaven is like a certain king who wanted to settle accounts with his servants. And when he had begun to settle accounts, one was brought to him who owed him ten thousand talents. But as he was not able to pay, his master commanded that he be sold, with his wife and children and all that he had, and that payment be made. The servant therefore fell down before him, saying, 'Master, have patience with me, and I will pay you all.' Then the master of that servant was moved with compassion, released him, and forgave him the debt.

But that servant went out and found one of his fellow servants who owed him a hundred denarii; and he laid hands on him and took *him* by the throat, saying, 'Pay me what you owe!' So his fellow servant fell down at his feet and begged him, saying, 'Have patience with me, and I will pay you all.' And he would not, but went and threw him into prison till he should pay the debt. So when his fellow servants saw what had been done, they were very grieved, and came and told their master all that had been done. Then his master, after he had called him, said to him, 'You wicked servant! I forgave you all that debt because you begged me. Should you not also have had compassion on your fellow servant, just as I had pity on you?' And his master was angry, and delivered him to the torturers until he should pay all that was due to him.

So My heavenly Father also will do to you if each of you, from his heart, does not forgive his brother his trespasses" (Matthew 18:21–35).

Peter wants to know how many times he must forgive his brother. Is seven times enough?

Jesus responds, "Up to seventy times seven." Now, Jesus wasn't trying to make Peter do a math equation. His point was not that you have to forgive someone 490 times, and then you're done. Rather, forgiveness is unlimited, especially when we understand how God has forgiven us.

Jesus tells a story of a servant (we will call him George) who owed his master "ten thousand talents" (v. 24). A talent was a massive amount of money—approximately 60–70 pounds of gold. One estimate places the talent's worth as high as $300,000. At that rate, ten thousand talents would equal $3 billion. Jesus is speaking of a bizarre amount of money that nobody could ever pay back.

George owed his master a $3 billion debt. His only option was to beg for mercy, knowing that he, his wife, and his children would otherwise be sold to pay the unpayable debt. George would have to work two hundred thousand years to pay off his debt. Incredibly, the master forgives him, and he is now debt-free. It is a miracle!

Debt-free George then goes to find one of his fellow servants (we will call him Sam) who owes him 100 denarii. That was equivalent to about three months' wages for a soldier or laborer at that time and probably worth about $10,000. You would think that a person who has been released from billions of dollars of debt would be in a forgiving mood. So it is very surprising when George grabs Sam by the throat and demands, "Pay me what you owe!" (v. 28) Sam does not have the money, so he asks for patience and promises to pay when he can. But instead of extending the same forgiveness he was shown, George throws Sam into prison until the debt is repaid.

When the master finds out what George did, he revokes the forgiveness of his debt and turns George over to the torturers. Then Jesus says, "So My heavenly Father also will do to you if each of you, from his heart, does not forgive his brother his trespasses" (v. 35). We realize that *torture* is a pretty strong word, but unforgiveness truly is a torturous lifestyle. Consider this except from a Johns Hopkins Medicine article titled "Forgiveness: Your Health Depends on It":

Unforgiveness truly is a torturous lifestyle.

> Chronic anger puts you into a fight-or-flight mode, which results in numerous changes in heart rate, blood pressure and immune response. Those changes, then, increase the risk of depression, heart disease and diabetes, among other conditions.[1]

There is nothing inherently wrong with anger. We all get angry, and it is inevitable that you will get angry sometimes in your life. The problem is when we do not deal with our anger. Ephesians 4:26–27 says, "'Be angry, and do not sin': do not let the sun go down on your wrath, nor give place to the devil." The word "devil" in this passage comes from *diabolos*, which means 'slanderous, accusing falsely.'[2] When you "let the sun go down on your wrath," you give an opening to the enemy who wants to bring division into your relationships and demonic torment into your life.

Unforgiveness can take many forms:

- revenge (murder, violence, abuse)

- hate

- verbal abuse (slander, gossip, sarcasm, labeling, name-calling)

- divorce

- rejection and avoidance for punishment's sake

- withholding good

- transference of affection

- prejudice, bigotry, racism, or sexism

- bitterness

- wishing for bad things to happen to someone

- praying against someone

What do these forms have in common? They're all petty in the eyes of God. The unforgiving servant (George) forgot his master's sacrifice, and we often do the exact same thing. Jesus was the most righteous person in the history of the world, and He died the worst death in the history of the world because our sins put Him there.

One of the bad things about unforgiveness is that much of the time, we actually feel good about it. We feel justified in our bitterness and bad behavior. We point to what a person has done and declare, "You just don't understand what they did! I would *never* do that!"

You may be accurate in that you would never repeat a certain wrongdoing, but we have *all* done bad things. Do we understand what we did to Jesus and what He had to endure because of us? Our sins put Jesus on the cross. Our wrongdoings hammered the nails, thrust the spear, cracked the whip, placed the crown of thorns, and nailed the sign mocking Him as the King of the Jews.

Someone may owe you the emotional equivalent of 100 denarii, but for what you did to Jesus, you owe Him billions of dollars. Make that trillions while you are at it. You could never begin to repay even the interest on what you owe Jesus. But He forgave you. Once you truly understand that, you will have a different attitude about everything, including forgiveness.

In Matthew 23:37 Jesus mourns for Jerusalem and says, "How often I wanted to gather your children together, as a hen gathers her chicks under *her* wings, but you were not willing!" As a child, I (Jimmy) spent my summers on my grandfather's farm, and twice a day I had to gather eggs from 500 chickens. I can tell you that I quickly learned to leave a hen with her chicks alone. Hens are the most protective animals; when those little chicks run under their mother's wings, the hen is ready for war. She will peck your face off!

Love and forgiveness are God's property. When you are walking in forgiveness, you are walking under His covering. Hate, on the other hand, is the devil's territory. If you refuse to forgive, you walk out from under God's wings and onto Satan's property. You expose yourself to torture and torment.

Unforgiveness will always hurt your relationship with the Lord. In Matthew 6:15, Jesus says, "If you do not forgive men their trespasses, neither will your Father forgive your trespasses." Unforgiveness is a *huge* deal! God will not forgive our sins if we do not forgive others. This is one of the reasons why Jesus includes forgiveness in the Lord's Prayer. Matthew 6:12 says, "And forgive us our debts, as we forgive our debtors." Forgiveness needs to be a daily prayer because the opportunity for unforgiveness is a daily occurrence. People will always do things that upset us, and most of us have endured deep hurts in our past. If we don't deal with our upsets and hurts, they will produce bitterness, hate, and unforgiveness.

Unforgiveness will always hurt your relationship with the Lord.

Disarm the Torpedo

Unforgiveness is a torpedo that launches from your past, destroys your present, and erases your future. You need to disarm it before it can do any further damage to you and, by extension, your child.

We encourage you to make a list of everyone from your past that you haven't forgiven. Ask the Holy Spirit to remind you of anyone you may have forgotten about that you need to forgive. This could be parents, stepparents, siblings, friends, neighbors, teachers, coaches, bosses, business partners, spouses, ex-spouses, ex-lovers, children, relatives, and more. Be sure to make your list complete.

We are now going to lead you in a three-step process of forgiveness for the people on your list. You may have to repeat these steps a number of times for those who really hurt you, but don't stop until you receive a breakthrough and know it is resolved. You cannot afford unforgiveness in your life. Your child can't afford unforgiveness in your life. Take a deep breath, and let's begin.

1. Repent of unforgiveness

If you have harbored long-term anger or bitterness toward someone, then the first step is to repent to God. You see, unforgiveness isn't merely a problem to be solved—it is a sin against Him. Our sins put Jesus on the cross. On that cross, Jesus forgave those who put Him there and died so our sins could be forgiven. He literally shut the doors of hell and opened the gates of heaven for us through His death. And what He requires of us in return is that we forgive others in the same spirit by which we have been forgiven by

God. When we won't, it is a sin against God and His grace. Repent and ask God to forgive you, and He will.

2. Release the offender from your judgment

When you forgive, you're entrusting God with the person who offended you, trusting that His judgments are correct. Then, it is up to God to deal with that individual. Harboring unforgiveness is the same as telling God you don't trust Him, His intelligence, or His character when it comes to dealing with that other person. Bitterness stems from a spirit that demands justice before you are willing to move on. Remember, if you want justice from someone else, it means you are also under that same justice. Don't hope someone gets "what they deserve"—you don't want what you deserve in the court of God's justice. Give grace and mercy and trust the rest to God.

3. Bless the offender until your feelings toward them change

Jesus said, "Love your enemies, do good to those who hate you, bless those who curse you, and pray for those who spitefully use you" (Luke 6:27–28). You can't fight fire with fire unless you just want a bigger fire. When you fight hate with hate, expect more hate. The only way to defeat a negative spirit in your life is with the opposite spirit. If someone did something wrong to you, go before God and bless that person. Bless them until the negative spirit is off you.

As you go through the process of blessing people who have hurt you, things may not change immediately. It might take you weeks, months, or even a few months. Nevertheless, the day is coming when you will be praying, obeying God, and fighting a negative spirit with the opposite spirit, and the Lord is going to do a deep healing in your heart. It will be like draining an infection out of you. The devil will lose the open door that he has used to oppress you.

As a pastor's kid, I (Julie) had plenty of opportunities growing up to learn about forgiveness, but as a parent, it is especially difficult to forgive when other people hurt my children. My husband, Cory, and I sent our two girls to a small, private Christian school for several years, and there was a tight-knit group of women that I think could be appropriately labeled "helicopter moms." They were into *everyone's* business, and they intimidated anyone who didn't do things their way. I never expected to experience peer pressure as an adult, especially not from other believers, and I couldn't believe these women were trying to intimidate my daughters and me. For a little while, I thought, *Maybe their way is the right way*, but thankfully, Cory and I figured out that we were only responsible to God for how we led our family. We had to do what we felt was right for our family, even if it meant going against popular opinion.

One particular woman was the ringleader of the mom group, and she did a lot of emotional damage to our family. The pain she caused me was bad enough, but the pain she caused my daughters made me hurt even more. It was incredibly difficult, but I wanted to be obedient to the Lord, so I made the choice to forgive her and the other moms, and we even let them back into our lives after a little while. But then this woman did the same hurtful things again! Sadly, she hadn't changed, and Cory and I realized that for the health and safety of our family, we had to forgive her *and* remove ourselves from that relationship.

Recently my daughters and I were talking about that private school, and they made the comment, "You're so forgiving. We can't believe you were able to forgive those moms." I was surprised! I knew my daughters had been hurt by that situation, but I didn't know they had been watching my words and actions. I realized that forgiveness wasn't just an act of obedience in my relationship with God, but it also had a lasting impact on our family.

Some wounds go very deep, and I still have to make the choice every day to forgive those moms and not allow bitterness to take root in my heart. If you are struggling with unforgiveness, I want to recommend two resources for you: *21 Day Total Freedom Journey* and *21 Day Inner Healing Journey*. My dad is the author, and he shares stories, Scriptures, confessions, and prayers to help you learn to close the door on the pain of unforgiveness and find healing and freedom in God's Word.

If you will obey God in blessing and praying for those who have offended you or those you love, He will be faithful to heal your emotions so you can go forward with a renewed heart. As you bless others, He will bless you.

7

FREE TO FIGHT

Understanding the importance of forgiveness is a crucial step toward freedom. Just as your child won't be more spiritual than you, it's also true that your child won't be more free than you. In this chapter, we are going to examine iniquities and inner vows. You may or may not be familiar with these terms, but they are key factors in determining how free you are to fight for your child.

Iniquities

The concept of generational sin appears early in the Bible. Adam and Eve's sin ("the Fall") has affected every generation of people on this planet. Even though we weren't in the Garden of Eden and didn't eat the forbidden fruit with them, we nevertheless suffer because of their sin.

The same truth applies to our parents. Their behavior, whether good or bad, has a profound impact on us. When our parents are righteous, they have a positive impact upon us. However, when they are sinful and wrong, the result is an unrighteous influence upon our lives, which often results in the same sin. (Even when we don't follow our parents' sin, our lives are still influenced negatively.) The Bible calls this family dynamic "iniquities."

Here is what the Lord says:

"The LORD, the LORD God, merciful and gracious, longsuffering, and abounding in goodness and truth, keeping mercy for thousands, forgiving **iniquity** and transgression and sin, by no means clearing *the guilty*, visiting the iniquity of the fathers upon the children and the children's children to the third and the fourth generation" (Exodus 34:6–7, bold added).

The word "iniquity" comes from the Hebrew verb *avah*, which means 'to bend, twist.'[1] An iniquity is a bent toward sin that comes from our parents. Remember the saying, "The acorn doesn't fall far from the tree"? In Deuteronomy 5:9, God says He visits "the iniquity of the fathers upon the children to the third and fourth *generations*." Mothers aren't off the hook, though. The word "fathers" in this verse can also be translated "ancestors," thereby including both sexes.

No one has perfect parents, and there are many common iniquities, such as:

- fear
- dominance
- rebellion
- materialism
- anger
- legalism

- sexism
- gossip
- racism
- pride
- laziness
- unforgiveness

- negativity
- substance abuse
- stubbornness
- verbal abuse
- divorce
- physical abuse

Now, you don't have to have your parents' help to sin—we all do quite fine sinning on our own. But iniquities are generationally trained sins. Children see a behavior every day while they are growing up, and it becomes ingrained in them. Abusive or dominant behavior is frequently learned from parents and generational family systems. I (Jimmy) came from generations of dominant males who bent me in the wrong direction toward chauvinism. And I (Karen) had a dominant father *and* a dominant mother who bent me in the wrong direction toward anger and shame.

The proper way to address conflict is to speak the truth in love, express emotions, and forgive. But when I (Jimmy) was growing up, that is not how my family did things. Instead, we gave each other "the silent treatment." You knew someone was over being mad at you when they would look at you and speak to you again.

I (Karen) had the opposite type of family. We would shout and argue and say mean things, but then just a short while later, we would be hugging and saying we loved each other. So imagine the chaos and confusion when Jimmy and I got married. I would yell at him, and he wouldn't talk to me for three or four days. We were poster children for how to do conflict all wrong. It was awful, and we were both sinning, but our parents had given us special training in how to do it.

Breaking Free from Iniquities

Without intervention, iniquities will always pass on to the next generation. They are built-in features, similar to genetics. The same is true for inner vows, which we will discuss in the next section. However, unlike genetics, iniquities (and inner vows) can be broken. You don't have to be tied to the pain of your family's past anymore.

> **Without intervention, iniquities will always pass on to the next generation.**

When we (Jimmy and Karen) finally figured out to how to be married God's way, we decided the two of us we would be the end of all iniquities in our families. We didn't want to transfer anything negative to our children or grandchildren. We wanted our iniquities to be broken, and in their place, we want to transfer God's "graciousness *and* lovingkindness to thousands [of generations]" (Deuteronomy 5:10 AMP). As we fought for the souls of our children, this was one battle we refused to lose.

Here are four steps to breaking free from iniquities:

1. **Recognize the iniquities of your parents.**

   An iniquity is any form of behavior you recognize in your parents' lives or family history as being unbiblical, failing to represent of the character of God, and having a generational influence.

2. **Forgive your parents (and anyone else who modeled that behavior for you).**

   You must forgive your parents and realize that whatever baggage they handed you was probably also handed to them.

3. **Repent and submit this area of your life to Jesus Christ.**

   Pray, "Lord, I repent of this tendency, and I submit it to you." Jesus will disciple and train you, and He will straighten you from your bent in this area.

4. **Break the devil off the iniquity.**

   Declare, "In the name of Jesus, I break this iniquity over my life." If you're really struggling in an area, talk to someone you can trust, such as a fellow believer, pastor, or Christian counselor. James 5:16 says, "Confess *your* trespasses to one another, and pray for one another, that you may be healed. The effective, fervent prayer of a righteous man avails much."

The reason sin destroys families is because we fail to recognize it and deal with it properly. However, if we will call sin what it is, forgive those who have sinned, and repent of our own sins, the blood of Jesus erases the power of that sin from our lives. Your iniquities can be broken, and you will be set free.

Inner Vows

My (Jimmy's) dad worked all the time when I was growing up, even more than his boss required of him. I always thought it was odd and just assumed my dad was a workaholic. (I eventually had the same tendency.)

My dad never explained his behavior, but when I was an adult, his sisters (my aunts) shared the truth about their past. My dad had nine brothers and sisters, and they all grew up in total poverty. My dad slept outside on a cot because there was only one bedroom in the house. In the winter, he slept with the horses to stay warm. Meat was a once-a-week luxury.

My dad didn't realize he came from a poor family until he went to school for the first time. Looking around, he saw that everyone else was wearing shoes while his feet were bare. Other children had shirts, but he only had overalls. My dad was so embarrassed that he ran outside, grabbed a tree, and refused to let go until his parents came to the school to get him. That experience shamed my dad, and right then and there, he made himself a promise: "My children will always have shoes."

Inner vows are promises we make to ourselves, often in response to pain, difficulty, or frustration. Here are some common examples of inner vows:

- "No one will ever hurt me again."
- "I'm never going to trust anyone else in my life."
- "I'm not going to be strict with my children."
- "When I get older, I will always ..."

We make inner vows to comfort ourselves relative to the future. We aren't trying to do something wrong or evil; rather, we are trying to prevent wrong or evil from happening again. However, regardless of how noble our motive is, there are three major problems with inner vows.

They are unscriptural

"You have heard that it was said to those of old, 'You shall not swear falsely, but shall perform your oaths to the Lord.' But I say to you, do not swear at all: neither by heaven, for it is God's throne; nor by the earth, for it is His footstool; nor by Jerusalem, for it is the city of the great King. Nor shall you swear by your head, because you cannot make one hair white or black. But let your 'Yes' be 'Yes,' and your 'No,' 'No.' For whatever is more than these is from the evil one" (Matthew 5:33–37).

Jesus clearly tells us that we shouldn't be swearing anything to ourselves or anyone else. He then reveals that it is from the evil one. You might wonder, *Why is it so wrong for me to make an inner vow or to swear to something?* Because in any area we swear to ourselves, Jesus isn't the Lord of that area—we are.

In any area we swear to ourselves, Jesus isn't the Lord of that area—we are.

Jesus tells us to "perform your oaths to the Lord." If we are going to make any significant commitments in our lives, they are to be focused toward God and fulfilled as an act of worship and obedience to Him. Inner vows are the exact opposite—they are self-focused, self-serving promises that in many cases resist and oppose the will of God in our lives. It is possible for Christians to live their entire lives with multiple inner vows operating under the surface of their consciousness while living with the impression that they are completely submitted to the Lord.

They have an unseen effect

When inner vows are directing your life, God isn't. For example, if someone has made an inner vow never to be poor again, they are then obligated to themselves to fulfill that vow. Suddenly, they have become the god of their finances. Some of the greediest, most materially driven people we have ever known were fulfilling their inner vows from the past.

When you are operating under the influence of an inner vow, you are unteachable, unapproachable, and irrational. You become incredibly fearful and hypervigilant to anything you think might threaten your vow. I (Jimmy) had a friend who drank more soft drinks than any other person I've ever known. He spent so much money stockpiling soda in his house that he and his wife fought about it. I later found out that when my friend was growing up, his mother did not allow any sodas in the house. So as a teenager, my friend made this inner vow: "When I grow up, I'm going to have a Coke machine in my living room. They will be free for anyone who comes to my house and wants to get a soft drink." And he kept that vow, and no one could talk him out of it.

They are our highest level of commitment

Our greatest commitment should be to the Lord, but when we promise ourselves that we will or will or not do something, that promise subconsciously overrides any commitment to Him. This point is why there are many precious, sincere Christians who say they love God but have so many areas of their lives operating in such opposition to His purposes. Without even realizing it, they are fulfilling an inner vow that has become a competitor with Christ.

Take the example of "No one is ever going to hurt me again." I (Jimmy) once counseled a married couple, and the husband had never let his wife into his home. Yes, you read that correctly. He lived in a house, and she rented an apartment. Obviously, this piqued my interest, and I asked the loaded question: "Why?" The man said he had a very dominant mother who "emasculated" his father daily. As a boy, the husband made this vow: "No woman will ever treat me like that." I shocked him when I said, "You're doing the same thing to your wife. Whatever your mother did to your father, you're a whole lot worse than that to your wife."

Breaking Free from Inner Vows

With inner vows, we go from one extreme to another. These vows keep us in bondage, and the enemy would love for you to think, *It's not a big deal* so you can continue sabotaging your life, your relationships, and God's destiny for you. But until you renounce your inner vows and submit them to God, you won't find the peace you are looking for in life.

Ask the Holy Spirit to show you any inner vows in your life. Sometimes we forget because there is pain attached, but He will show you. Then follow these four steps:

1. **Renounce the inner vow.**

   You may have made it in total innocence, but now you know it's a sin. Pray something like this:

   > *I renounce this vow I made to myself. I didn't realize it was wrong, but I do now. I repent for making a vow to myself and not turning this area of my life over to You, Lord. From this day forward, the vow is null and void and will not direct my speech or actions.*

2. **Submit that area of your life to the Lord.**

   It is important for us to submit the vow to the Lord and become teachable and approachable. It is also important to become teachable and approachable to others in our lives, such as our parents, our spouses, and authority figures. Take a moment to ensure every area in which you made an inner vow is now under the authority of Jesus. Also, pray for a teachable and approachable spirit toward others.

3. **Forgive everybody associated with the vow.**

   Forgive ex-spouses, parents, children, ex-business partners, or anyone else who was involved. Take some time to pray about forgiveness for each person. Repeat the prayer as often as necessary until you feel total release and freedom.

4. **Bind and cast out the evil one.**

When you made those vows, you chose to become your own god, and everything went off track. You must take authority over it in Jesus' name. Break the spiritual power of each vow and bind every spirit associated with it.

> *Lord, in Jesus' name I break the power of the inner vow that I spoke. I bind every demon spirit that used my vow to harass, deceive, or control me. Thank you, God, for forgiving me of the sin of making the vow, and I place myself under Your authority and covering. I declare that I am free! In Jesus' name, Amen.*

Breaking free from iniquities and inner vows isn't a casual pastime. No, it's an act of war. Refuse to let yourself or anyone in your family be held captive by the enemy any longer. If you would like more information on iniquities or inner vows, *21 Day Total Freedom Journey* will help you tremendously. You can find freedom in Jesus Christ, and when you do, you will truly be free to fight for the soul of your child.

8

Chain of Command

In every military organization, there is a structure called the chain of command that determines how military personnel relate to each other. It is a top-down structure, which means the higher a person's rank, the more priority and authority—the more power—he or she has. Generals have more power than lieutenants, lieutenants have more power than sergeants, etc. Following the chain of command is nonnegotiable, particularly in times of war. Insubordination will result in disciplinary action, ranging from loss of privileges and pay to dishonorable discharge and court-martial.

Would it surprise you to learn that the kingdom of God has its own chain of command? Many people aren't aware that the Bible has clear instructions about the way and order in which we are supposed to relate to God and others. And these instructions are not a suggestion. No, they are the law of priority—emphasis on *law*—which affects everything we say and do.

When you obey God's law of priority, you place yourself directly under the protection of His Word.

When you obey God's law of priority, you place yourself directly under the protection of His Word. You are following His chain of command, and you have authority over the enemy. But when you decide on your own way of doing things, you lose your protection and authority. Your eternal salvation is still secure, but your day-to-day joy and peace are threatened.

The details of this law of priority aren't complicated. We are going to focus on the order of the first three links in God's chain of command, and they are as follows:

1. God

2. Spouse

3. Children

According to Scripture, this order is fixed; it's nonnegotiable. But that doesn't mean it's always easy. A parent can become so involved in fighting for their child that they forget to fight for their spouse, and suddenly the child and the spouse end up in the wrong order. As with inner vows, the intentions were good, but the wrong order will never produce the right outcome.

One way to understand the necessity of protecting priorities is to look at your time and energy as if they were money. Money is a limited asset, and you have to budget it in order to use it wisely. It would be foolish to spend all your money on luxuries and non-essentials and leave nothing for the rent or food. When the land-lord came to collect, how do you think he would respond if you said, "I can't pay you, but I really am a good tenant"? The same concept is true with time and energy. You must spend your time and energy wisely because they are precious, limited resources.

Let's take a deeper look at how God designed you to relate to Him, to your spouse, and to your child. (If you aren't married but would like to be someday, we encourage you to stick with us!)

God

Many people claim to love God first because they know it's the right or "Christian" thing to say, even though they spend very little time or attention on their relationship with Him. But God is omniscient—He knows everything, and He knows who loves Him first. He sees in real terms how we operate in every area of our lives, not just with our words or good intentions. In Exodus 34:14, He commands Israel, "Do not worship any other god, for the LORD, whose name is Jealous, is a jealous God" (NIV).

Jealousy is generally considered to be a negative motion. It's often used synonymously with envy, which is wanting what someone else has (something that doesn't belong to us). But jealousy, which can also be described as "zealous vigilance,"[1] is about protecting what is yours. Psalm 24:1 says, "The earth is the LORD's, and everything in it, the world, and all who live in it" (NIV). We belong to God, and He created us to love and serve Him *first*.

God passionately loves us and fights to protect the integrity of our relationship with Him.

Whenever we give time, energy, or resources that rightfully belong to Him to another person, project, or activity, He is provoked with legitimate jealousy. God will not share His throne—not with your job, your friends, your hobbies, your spouse, or even your children.

Loving people is important, and Scripture has a lot to say about how we treat each other. But even more important is loving God. We aren't asked to love Him first. Jesus said in John 14:15, "If you love Me, you will keep My commandments" (NASB). We are *commanded* to love Him first, above anyone and everything else.

How do you show God that you love Him first? You give Him the first (and best) of your day. Years ago, when the kids were very young, I (Karen) disciplined myself to get up an hour before anyone else and spend some time with God. We didn't have a spare bedroom, so I took a little pillow into the closet and sat in there as

I read my Bible and prayed. Was it easy getting up so early? No, but I truly felt that if I didn't spend time with God, I wouldn't make it through the day. I clung to Philippians 3:8, which says, "Yet indeed I also count all things loss for the excellence of the knowledge of Christ Jesus my Lord, for whom I have suffered the loss of all things, and count them as rubbish, that I may gain Christ."

Loving God means obeying His command to honor the Sabbath (see Exodus 20:8–11). One full day a week belongs to Him. And you know what else belongs to Him? The tithe—the first 10 percent of your income. We realize that people don't like to give up their hard-earned money, but when you understand that *everything* you have comes from God, you realize that it's not *your* money. Plus, obedience is such a small price to pay for His blessings in your life (see Malachi 3:10–12).

Loving God isn't about perfection—it's about sacrifice. And no matter what we give up, be it time, energy, or money, there's no sacrifice we could make that would ever equal the sacrifice Jesus made on the cross for us. Only through Him can we have a relationship with our heavenly Father.

Loving God isn't about perfection— it's about sacrifice.

When you wake up every day and have a relationship with God, He heals you and gives you wisdom and strength. He solves problems that nobody else can solve. It's amazing how petty we as people can be under pressure, but with the power of the Holy Spirit, it is amazing how godly we can be under pressure.

Spouse

God designed marriage to operate as the most important human relationship in our lives, second only to our relationship with Him.

This doesn't mean your parents, siblings, friends, and children else are unimportant, but it does mean that your spouse takes precedence over them. Genesis 2:24 says, "Therefore shall a man leave his father and his mother, and shall cleave unto his wife: and they shall be one flesh" (Genesis 2:24 KJV). You and your spouse are *one*, and together, you have a 100 percent chance of success in marriage if you do it God's way.

Sadly, there are countless couples whose relationships have ended in divorce because one or both spouses allowed something to usurp the priority of their marriage. There are also millions of couples who stayed together but have frustrated, strife-filled lives for the same reason. God made your marriage to get better with time, not worse, but this only happens if your spouse is above every other relationship (except for God).

In a marriage, both spouses have moral obligations to God and each other to keep their relationship from being violated by people or things of lesser priorities. When one spouse's time, energy, and resources that rightfully belong to the other are given to someone or something else in any consistent or significant way, the violated spouse will feel legitimate jealousy.

One of the biggest priority struggles couples must address is spouse versus children. Who gets the top spot after God? One day I (Jimmy) was watching a TV show about families. The wives were together in one room, and they didn't know that their husbands, who were gathered in a different room, could hear their conversation. These women all agreed, "Nothing is as important to me as my children." A casual listener might not see anything wrong with such a statement. After all, it seems like a wholesome thing for a mother to say. But to their husbands, the wives' words were devastating. The men felt frustrated, bitter, and violated. Why? Because they had lost their wives to their children. It was a competition they didn't realize they were in until they discovered they couldn't win.

Of course, misplaced priorities are not just a mom issue. Dads do the same thing, bumping their child above their spouse or even above God. Our society desperately needs dads who will be involved with their children, but not at the expense of their relationship with God and their wives. If you think nothing is as important as your children, you're wrong. Two things are more important: God and your marriage.

When one parent begins to prioritize the children over the spouse, the violated spouse often turns their attention to their career or other interests outside the home. At this point, no one is prioritizing the marriage. If you allow anything or anyone, no matter how good or important, to take the time and energy that rightfully belongs to your spouse, you are violating God's design for marriage.

We (Jimmy and Karen) made so many mistakes for the first several years of our marriage. We were the classic American couple who married for love but didn't have a clue as to how marriage worked. I (Jimmy) was the husband who spent his energy at work, and if I was not working, I played golf every time I got a chance. Meanwhile, I (Karen) was the wife who spent all her time and effort on the children. We fought about our priorities all the time, and our relationship became more defensive and self-destructive every year. We couldn't even talk about our problems without getting into an argument.

One night we had a huge fight that ended with me (Jimmy) telling Karen to get out of the house and out of my life. Our marriage could have been over right then. But as Karen cried in the bedroom, the Holy Spirit reminded me of a Scripture I had read that very morning: "But the Advocate, the Holy Spirit, whom the Father will send in my name, will teach you all things and will remind you of everything I have said to you" (John 14:26 NIV). I got on my knees and asked God to teach me how to be a husband.

I didn't hear an audible voice, but I did hear God speak clearly to my heart. There was no doubt about it: I had put myself, my job, and golf above Karen. When I admitted my mistakes and apologized to her, the healing in our marriage began. Karen also apologized to me for mistakes she had made, and I forgave her. Since that time, we have never forgotten the importance of keeping each other first. As a result, I can say that every year of our marriage since then has been better than the year before. We are much more in love today, and we know how to love each other better than we did in the beginning. That is how God intended marriage to be.

Child

After your relationship with God and your relationship with your spouse, your children are the most important thing in your life. Psalm 127:3 says, "Children are a gift from the LORD; they are a reward from him" (NLT). Your children should come before work, church, hobbies, extended family members, friends, etc. Sometimes this can be difficult for parents who work in vocational ministry because they confuse "work" and "church" with God. Your relationship with God always comes first. But your job and your church involvement come *after* your spouse and your children.

Back when I (Jimmy) first started in ministry, there weren't cell phones, computers, or answering machines. I was a young pastor, and when our home phone would ring, I didn't know who it was. People called from the church all the time at all hours. It could be anything from someone needing me to open a door at the church to someone being in a crisis. I would answer the phone, and I could read my kids' faces: "Daddy's gone." So I unlisted my phone number, much to the frustration and offense of some of our church members. A few people even left the church altogether! I had submitted the idea to the elders, and it barely received their approval. But the people in the church simply weren't as important as my children. If caller ID had been around, that would have made a huge difference, but we simply didn't have that technology back then. I unlisted my phone number to protect my family.

In chapter 1, we shared that your purpose as a parent is to teach and train your child to know and love God. But did you know that you aren't the only one doing the teaching and training? Children learn everywhere they go, and their peers have more influence on them than parents could ever imagine. First Corinthians 15:33 says, "Do not be deceived: 'Bad company corrupts good morals'" (NASB). Parents, you need to know who your child's friends are and, if possible, who their friends' families are. If your child begins acting out, check out what is happening with their friends. You may need to put some boundaries around those relationships.

Something we (Jimmy and Karen) always said from the time our kids were very young is *no one has the right to play with our children.* It didn't matter to us if it was a cousin, a neighbor, or a child of one of our church members. If this person didn't have good character, they weren't going to be around our children. And this applied to the parents as well. Brent and Julie had some friends who were fine, but the parents weren't. We would let these friends come over to our house, but we wouldn't let our kids go to their home. The other parents were sometimes offended, but it was more important to us to protect our children.

No one has the right to play with our children.

Who are your children's friends? Who are their parents, and what do they believe? When Brent was 12 years old, he was invited to go see a movie with a friend. The friend's dad called me and assured me that he would be with the boys and that they would have a great time. I (Jimmy) thought, *Well, the dad is going, so I'm sure it will be fine.* But this dad took the boys to an R-rated movie! When Brent came home and told me what movie they had seen, I was shocked. Karen and I would never have allowed him to see that! I had made the mistake of trusting the judgment of the other parent without knowing him well enough, and believe me—that was a mistake I did *not* repeat!

We (Jimmy and Karen) were not perfect parents by any means, but our goal was to protect the time and energy intended for our kids from lesser priorities. In addition to regular meals where we sat around the table and talked, we spent time with our children regularly. We took family vacations. We went to church as a family. And at night, we prayed with the kids when we put them to bed. All this togetherness meant we had to say no to a lot of other things, but we never regretted the time spent with our children.

God created the law of priority to protect your relationship with Him and your relationship with your family. The greatest threats to these relationships aren't bad things—they're good things out of priority. We are not anti-work, anti-hobbies, or anti-friends, and we certainly aren't anti-church. But God must come first. Your spouse must come second. And your children must come third.

In this first section, we have addressed the rules of engagement when it comes to fighting for the soul of your child.

- We have determined the purpose of parenting and your child's most important needs.
- We have examined the soul and its enemy.
- We have explored the importance of salvation, forgiveness, and the breaking free of iniquities and inner vows.
- We have studied the chain of command and seen how crucial it is to obey the law of priority.

We encourage you to refer to these chapters as often as necessary because they provide the foundation every parent needs as they prepare to go into battle for their child.

Now, take a deep breath, stretch if you need to, and let's get back to work. We are going to take a deep dive into the whats and whys of godly parenting. You will figure out what you really believe about God, yourself, and the enemy, and you will discover how to protect and connect with your children. You may feel stretched or even convicted as you read, but that's okay. Boot camp was never meant to be easy.

SECTION 2

BOOT CAMP

9

A Biblical Worldview

In the parable of the Ten Virgins, Jesus prophesies about the falling away of half the Church in the end times:

> "Then the kingdom of heaven shall be likened to ten virgins who took their lamps and went out to meet the bridegroom. Now five of them were wise, and five *were* foolish. Those who were foolish took their lamps and took no oil with them, but the wise took oil in their vessels with their lamps. But while the bridegroom was delayed, they all slumbered and slept.
>
> And at midnight a cry was heard: 'Behold, the bridegroom is coming; go out to meet him!' Then all those virgins arose and trimmed their lamps. And the foolish said to the wise, 'Give us some of your oil, for our lamps are going out.' But the wise answered, saying, 'No, lest there should not be enough for us and you; but go rather to those who sell, and buy for yourselves.' And while they went to buy, the bridegroom came, and those who were ready went in with him to the wedding; and the door was shut.
>
> Afterward the other virgins came also, saying, 'Lord, Lord, open to us!' But he answered and said, 'Assuredly, I say to you, I do not know you.'
>
> Watch therefore, for you know neither the day nor the hour in which the Son of Man is coming" (Matthew 25:1–13).

In this parable, the bridegroom represents Jesus, and the virgins are symbolic of the Church. Jesus is effectively saying, "When I appear, only half of the Church will be prepared for My return." This situation is happening right now, before our eyes.

Fighting for your child's soul is more than having your child repeat the sinner's prayer after you. Now, please don't misunderstand what we are saying. Salvation is the greatest gift we have ever been offered, and a child doesn't have to understand all the complexities of Christianity to know that they are a sinner in need of a Savior. However, some parents are so eager for their children to get saved that they find themselves trying to be the Holy Spirit, attempting to convict their children of sin and create heart change through behavior modification. As much as we love our children, we have to realize that we are not the fourth member of the Trinity. And while children do need correction, guidance, and discipline as we continually point them toward Jesus, there is only one Holy Spirit who can soften their hearts and open their eyes to their need for salvation.

> # As much as we love our children, we have to realize that we are not the fourth member of the Trinity.

It is a wonderful moment when a child truly understands the need for Jesus as Lord and Savior and is willing to surrender their life to Him. Leading your child through a prayer for salvation will be a life-changing experience for you both. But your child becoming a Christian doesn't mean your work is done.

Have you ever heard the phrase, "To know him is to love him"? The enemy wants to stop children from knowing God, because if they really know Him, they will love Him. By the way, there's a difference between *knowing about* someone and really knowing them. Plenty of people claim to know God, but whomever (or whatever) they know is not the God of the Bible. Satan will do everything he can to prevent your child from surrendering his or her life to the

Lord, but if that fails, he will do everything he can to steal the joy and victory that come from truly knowing and loving God.

This is why it's so important for every godly parent to teach their child a biblical worldview. A worldview is something that everyone has, even if they don't quite know what it means. One of the best definitions we've found is from Dr. George Barna, Director of Research and cofounder of the Cultural Research Center (CRC) at Arizona Christian University (ACU). Dr. Barna has studied the topic of worldview for more than 30 years, and he explains it this way:

> Worldview is the operating system for human beings. It tells us how to think and how to behave. It informs and directs the choices that we make…. Whenever we are about to make a decision, we unconsciously run it through a mental, spiritual and emotional filter that allows us to make choices consistent with what we believe to be true, significant and appropriate. That filter is the result of the information and experiences we have embraced to make sense of the world in which we live.[1]

If a worldview determines how we operate in daily life, then a biblical worldview determines our daily operations according to the Bible. Dr. Barna's research uses this definition of a biblical worldview:

> The biblical worldview is a means of experiencing, interpreting, and responding to reality in light of biblical perspectives. This view provides a personal understanding of every idea, opportunity, and experience based on the identification and application of relevant biblical principles so that each choice we make may be consistent with God's principles and commands. At the risk of seeming simplistic, it is asking the question, "What would Jesus do if He were in my shoes right now?" and applying the answer without concern for how we anticipate the world will react.

A biblical worldview is thinking like Jesus. It is a way of making our faith practical to every situation we face each day. A biblical worldview is a way of dealing with the world such that we act like Jesus, twenty-four hours a day, because we think like Jesus. Here's a helpful analogy: "It's like having a pair of special eyeglasses we wear that enables us to see things from God's point of view, and to respond to those perceptions in the way that He would prescribe if He were to provide us with direct and personal revelation."[2]

The CRC at ACU conducts an *American Worldview Inventory (AWVI)* to examine the worldview of adults in the United States. They ask more than 50 questions and use the following categories of belief to measure worldview:

- Bible, Truth, and Morals

- Faith Practices

- Family and the Value of Life

- God, Creation, and History

- Human Character and Nature

- Lifestyle, Behavior, and Relationships

- Purpose and Calling

- Sin, Salvation, and God Relationship[3]

Behavior is distinctly and directly impacted by one's worldview. Adults without a biblical worldview are more likely to accept cohabitation, condone homosexuality, use profanity, and find exposure to pornography morally acceptable.[4] They are less likely to believe that absolute moral truth exists, that God is involved in our lives, and that human beings were created by God in His image.

These were some of the troubling statistics from the CRC 2023 AWVI:

- 68 percent of American adults claim to be Christians, but only 6 percent have a biblical worldview.

- 33 percent of Americans are theologically defined born-again Christians, but only 13 percent of this population has a biblical worldview.

- Only 1 percent of adults under 30 years old have a biblical worldview.

- Only 3 percent of 30–40-year-old adults have a biblical worldview.

- Only 5 percent of 50–64-year-old adults have a biblical worldview.[5]

Here is what Dr. Barna had to say about the 2023 results:

> Biblical theism is much closer to extinction in America than it is to influencing the soul of the nation. The current incidence of adults with the biblical worldview is the lowest since I began measuring it in the early 1990s.... Young people, in particular, are largely isolated from biblical thought in our society and are the most aggressive at rejecting biblical principles in our culture. Facilitating a return to biblical thinking and living in America will take an intentional, strategic, and consistent effort by the remaining population that represents this biblical approach to life.[6]

These numbers are alarming. Not only do they indicate that the number of Bible-believing Christians is declining in our culture but also that many of those who *think* they are Christians aren't really Christians at all. The ancient Greeks used the word *nomizo* to refer to beliefs people held purely out of custom—for example, faith inherited from family members. We suspect that many in our society call themselves Christians because their parents were Christians, or because they attended a Christian church as a child. But they don't actually hold Christian beliefs. Their faith may be a *nomizo* kind of faith and not a genuine one.

In the Sermon on the Mount, Jesus said the "gate" into His Kingdom is a narrow one, but "broad *is* the way that leads to destruction" (Matthew 7:13). That broad path will be filled with atheists and agnostics, to be sure, and people who follow false religions. But it will also be filled with *nomizo* Christians.

Many people who attend church may not actually know Jesus.

Many people who attend church may not actually know Jesus. Many of them think they are followers of Christ but will be left behind in the Rapture. Dr. Barna has strong words of warning for parents today:

> Insanity would explain the way that parents raise their children then feel surprised when their youngsters become adults with different values and lifestyles.... A parent's primary responsibility is to prepare a child for the life God intends for that child. A crucial element in that nurturing is helping the child develop a biblical worldview—the filter that causes a person to make their choices in harmony with biblical teachings and principles.... The typical American parent is either fully unaware that there is a worldview development process, or they are aware that their child is developing a worldview, but they do not take responsibility for a role in the process.... Or they are aware the child's worldview is being developed, but choose or allow outsiders to accomplish that duty on the parent's behalf.... It seems that most pre-teen parents are unaware—or certainly unfazed—by the contradiction between calling themselves "Christian" but living in ways that repudiate the teachings of Jesus and the principles in the Bible....
>
> Shockingly few parents intentionally speak to their children about beliefs and behavior based upon a biblical worldview. Perhaps the most powerful worldview lesson parents provide is through their own behavior, yet our studies consistently indicate that parental choices generally do not reflect biblical principles or an intentionally Christian approach to life.[7]

Parents, this should be a wake-up call! We wonder why our children are struggling in school and relationships and even walking away from their faith when they become adults. It's easy to blame the growing momentum of faith deconstruction on secular universities, worldly influences, and fallen church leaders, and yes, these factors can play very significant roles. But before we point any fingers, we need to take a long look in the mirror. Have we followed the biblical mandate to teach and train our children to know and love God? Are we living out Deuteronomy 6:7 and diligently teaching God's Word to our children "when you sit in your house, when you walk by the way, when you lie down, and when you rise up"?

Again, it's not about legalism or perfection. There's no checklist in the Bible for parents to rate themselves on how many verses their children can recite or how many weekends in a row their family attends church. Yes, it's important to memorize Scripture and attend church, but these activities need to be birthed from relationship. We read the Bible because it helps us know and love the God who made us in His image. We attend church because it is a place to learn about and worship God *and* to build relationships with other people who know and love Him.

Obviously, there is a disconnect between the biblical command to raise our children according to God's Word and the present method of "Christian" parenting. Why is this? Dr. Barna offers a possible explanation:

> Parents these days often feel guilty "imposing" their views on their children, having bought into the notions that imparting inviolable guidelines to their children is overbearing and intolerant, and that it takes a village—which we know as our culture—to effectively raise a child these days.... That, of course, is antithetical to the God-given, biblical role of parents, which is to be the first and foremost shaper of the minds and hearts of their children toward bringing them under the authority of God.[8]

Let's be clear about something: Our culture is not going to fight for the soul of your child. Not in the way you want, anyway. And even if you have a strong network of faith-filled family and friends, it's still your responsibility to teach and train your child to know and love God. This is discipleship, or as author and pastor Tedd Tripp calls it, "spiritual nurturing":

> What your children need is spiritual nurture. They need to be taught the ways of God. They need to be instructed in the character of God so that they can learn a proper fear of God. They need to understand that all of life rushes toward the day when we shall stand before God and give account....You must always hold out to your children both their need for Christ's invasive redemptive work and their obligation to repent of their sin and place their faith in Jesus Christ. Repentance and faith are not rites of initiation to Christianity. Repentance and faith are the way to relate to God. Repentance and faith are not acts performed one time to become a Christian. They are attitudes of the heart toward ourselves and our sin. Faith is not just the way to get saved; it is the lifeline of Christian living.[9]

We recognize that parenting today takes so much faith. We live in a culture where absolutes are considered hateful and oppressive, and biblical principles are under attack like never before. Our children are being told that right and wrong are merely social constructs. There is even a new Bible app that encourages people to "ditch toxic theology" and "find your way to the spiritual wellness you deserve."[10]

We fully acknowledge that there are people who have been legitimately hurt by leaders in the Church, and we have deep compassion for anyone who is trying to navigate their way through false teachings to the actual truth of God's Word. But what concerns us is the growing movement to label anything people don't like or understand as "toxic." The world wants to disregard sections of the Bible that it deems offensive or old-fashioned, and this arrogant attitude is seeping into the Church. It's not a surprise to God, of course, and even the apostle Paul wrote, "For the message of the cross is foolishness to those who are perishing, but to us who are being saved it is the power of God" (1 Corinthians 1:18).

You know what's actually toxic? Sin. It has a 100 percent infection rate, and no one is immune. It's not up to society to determine who is a "good" person or what they "deserve," because society isn't the judge—God is. He is perfect, holy, and just, and "we all fall short of God's glorious standard" (Romans 3:23 NLT). If left to our own devices, we would all be doomed to eternal separation from our Creator.

This is why we so desperately and completely need a Savior, and this is what makes the Gospel so incredible. Jesus said, "I am the way, the truth, and the life. No one can come to the Father except through me" (John 14:6 NLT). In the New Testament, the people who rejected Jesus were the religious leaders who thought they could come to God through their own good works. And it's this same "I can save myself" ideology that is running rampant today. Here's what the Bible has to say about that:

> We are all infected and impure with sin.
>> When we display our righteous deeds,
>> they are nothing but filthy rags.
> Like autumn leaves, we wither and fall,
>> and our sins sweep us away like the wind (Isaiah 64:6 NLT).

We explained earlier that the armor of God is not an à la carte menu, and neither is the Bible. We cannot handpick the Scriptures that make us feel good (like "God is love" in 1 John 4:8) and reject the ones that make us feel uncomfortable. Jesus said, "If any of you wants to be my follower, you must give up your own way, take up your cross daily, and follow me. If you try to hang on to your life, you will lose it. But if you give up your life for my sake, you will save it" (Luke 9:23–24 NLT).

Holding a biblical worldview doesn't mean you claim to be a Bible expert or have no questions about theological topics. And it doesn't mean you will be a perfect parent. Rather, it means that you committed to living your life and raising your children with the Word of God as your standard and Jesus Christ as your Lord and Savior.

10

Who Am I?

Les Misérables, the classic Victor Hugo novel that became a hit Broadway musical, is the story of Jean Valjean, a poor French inmate who is released on parole after serving 19 years for stealing bread for his starving family. Jean Valjean tries to begin a new life, but a determined police inspector is always just one step behind him. One day, Jean Valjean learns that the police have arrested another man whom they believe to be him. This is his chance to be free! But it would mean that an innocent man would have his life destroyed, and Jean Valjean could never be himself again. In the Broadway adaptation, Jean Valjean weighs the pros and cons and searches his soul to determine, as the scene's song is aptly titled, "Who am I?"

This question is one that every person asks during their lifetime, and many people ask it multiple times. *Who am I?* To a casual observer, you are your name, your age, and your physical features. But to yourself and anyone who knows you well, there is so much more. You have personality traits, you have preferences, you have a purpose, etc. All these factors (and more) add up to a very powerful word: *identity.*

So many people base their identity on their job, their education, their relationships, their political associations, etc. Children see this and follow suit, identifying themselves by their grades, their athletic ability, their artistic or musical talent, and, of course, their peer groups. None of these factors are bad or evil in and of themselves, but they are all variable—they can change. What happens when a child who normally gets good grades fails a test, or a star athlete gets injured and can't play? What happens when a child's peers decide they no longer want to be friends with them? This can lead to an identity crisis for the child, just as losing a job might lead to an identity crisis for an adult.

Basing your identity on a variable factor opens the door for the enemy to feed disappointment, confusion, and heartache into your life whenever that factor changes. This is one reason why the law of priority is so crucial to follow. The way you identify yourself has to begin with your relationship with God before anyone else. Who does He say you are? Because God never changes, what He says never changes either. It is invariable. Discovering what God says about identity and teaching it to your children is one of the greatest gifts you can ever give them. We promise it will change their lives, just as it will change yours.

Because God never changes, what He says never changes either.

Identity in Christ

If you've been in an evangelical Christian church recently, you may have heard about "your identity in Christ." It sounds like a very spiritual phrase, right? It might surprise you to know that phrase doesn't come from the Bible, and it didn't become popular until the 1950s. Around that time, secular psychologists began focusing on identity in relation to personalities, gifts, and strengths, and Christian communicators picked up the phrase "identity in Christ" to focus on the need for believers to understand who they are in Jesus.

I (Jimmy) use the phrase "your identity in Christ" when I preach because people really do need to understand who they are in relation to Him so they can find freedom and inner healing. Satan is a liar who wants to keep us in bondage, but Jesus offers true freedom: "You are truly my disciples if you remain faithful to my teachings. And you will know the truth, and the truth will set you free" (John 8:31–32 NLT).

It's important to understand that your relationship with the Lord is so much more about Him than it is about you. In fact, instead of "your identity in Christ," a more biblical phrase is "your *union* in Christ." Your identity is most relevant when it is connected to Him. If you want to know who you are, then you need to know who God is and why He sent His Son, Jesus, so that you could be in eternal union with Him. Understanding who we are in Christ means we must first understand who He is.

In my book *Look Up!*, I teach a great deal about a believer's identity in Christ. I will share the key points here, but if you would like to do a deep dive into knowing God and yourself better, I highly recommend that book. Now, let's jump in.

When Jesus comes back in the Rapture, we will know exactly who God is and who we are in union with Him. In the meantime, we wait eagerly, prepare for His return, stay away from sin, and learn everything we can from and about Him. We will see and understand Him perfectly on the day Christ returns, and our eyes will be opened completely to our identity in Him. Right now, we must learn who God is and who we are in Jesus Christ. We are not left guessing. The Bible tells us who God is and who we are, and the Holy Spirit confirms it for us.

Who God Is

There are five ways the Bible describes God, and these ways run throughout the Bible from Genesis to Revelation. If we can understand how God reveals Himself, then we will better comprehend our identity in union with Him.

1. God is a Father.

He is intimately present for us, and we are His sons. First John 3:1 says, "Behold, what manner of love the Father hath bestowed upon us, that we should be called the sons of God!" (KJV).

2. God is a Bridegroom.

He wants us to be ready for Him when He comes, and He wants to have a deep, personal, and loving relationship with us. He is a Bridegroom, and we are His bride. (See John 3:29.)

3. God is a Messenger.

He freely delivers the gracious good news of His truth to us, and He wants us to tell others what He has said. God is a Messenger, and we are His prophets.

4. God is a Person.

He wants to give us access to Himself so we can receive forgiveness, bring others into His presence, and glorify Him. He is a Person, and we are His priests.

5. God is a King.

He is the Ruler of all Creation. Psalm 47:7 says, "For God *is* the King of all the earth." As King, He gives authority to His sons. God is a King, and He has made us kings to reign with Him.

The first human identity crisis happened in the Garden of Eden. God created Adam and Eve with a distinct identity to be what He wanted them to be and for them to do His will. But when they sinned, they lost their perfect relationship with God, and their identity was distorted. Thankfully, God did not give up on humans. Jesus Christ restores our relationship with God and enables us to reclaim our identity now both as individuals and as the Church. He will perfect that identity when He comes again because it is then that we will know Him perfectly.

In God's presence, we will finally see Him "as He is," and we will be like Him. At the Rapture, we will know Him perfectly and, in union with Christ, we will understand fully who we are.

Sons of God

You probably noticed that when we said God is our Father, we didn't say that believers are His *children*. Instead, we said that we are His sons. This is intentional. Did you realize that in the original Hebrew and Greek, women in the Bible were never referred to as "daughters of God"?[1] Now, we aren't saying you shouldn't think of yourself as God's daughter if you are a woman, but if you don't also see yourself as a son, then you are missing something very important.

In the ancient world, only sons received an inheritance, so the only way for a woman to gain wealth was to marry someone who had it. Daughters received nothing. If the writers of the Bible had originally said we are "sons and daughters of God," then women would have considered their current cultural situation and thought, *Well, I guess in the Kingdom of God, I still get nothing. I might be included, but I won't get an inheritance. It doesn't sound so great to me.*

When the Bible calls both men and women "sons of God," something profound is happening. It's a major statement about the worth of women in God's eyes. Keep that in mind when you see the term "sons of God" in the Bible. In God's Kingdom, women are sons too!

Look at what the apostle Paul says:

> I mean that the heir, as long as he is a child, is no different from a slave, though he is the owner of everything, but he is under guardians and managers until the date set by his father. In the same way we also, when we were children, were enslaved to the elementary principles of the world. But when the fullness of time had come, God sent forth his Son, born of woman, born under the law, to redeem those who were under the law, so that we might receive adoption as sons. And because you are sons, God has sent the Spirit of his Son into our hearts, crying, "Abba! Father!" So you are no longer a slave, but a son, and if a son, then an heir through God (Galatians 4:1–7 ESV).

Do you see what has happened? All of us—both men and women—were slaves to sin and the world. But God sent His own Son to pay the price for us to be adopted as sons of God. We can cry out, "Abba! Father!" *Daddy!* Can you believe it? This is an amazing inheritance!

Look at one more passage of Scripture from Paul:

> For all who are led by the Spirit of God are sons of God. For you did not receive the spirit of slavery to fall back into fear, but you have received the Spirit of adoption as sons, by whom we cry, "Abba! Father!" The Spirit himself bears witness with our spirit that we are children of God, and if children, then heirs—heirs of God and fellow heirs with Christ, provided we suffer with him in order that we may also be glorified with him (Romans 8:14–17 ESV).

You don't have to fear anymore. Jesus bought us out of slavery, our Father adopted us, and now we get a full inheritance. The Creator of the universe is your Dad, and you are His son.

The Creator of the universe is your Dad, and you are His son.

Identity in the New Testament

Here are some other ways the New Testament describes believers:[2]

> So now you Gentiles are no longer strangers and foreigners. You are citizens along with all of God's holy people. You are members of God's family (Ephesians 2:19 NLT).

You are not a stranger in God's house. You belong to Him and to all His people. Remember, you are now part of the family and a legitimate son of God.

And God will generously provide all you need. Then you will always have everything you need and plenty left over to share with others (2 Corinthians 9:8 NLT).

Since you are God's son, He will take care of you and give you everything you need in Christ. Everything belongs to God, so He can provide all you need.

For the LORD your God is living among you.
He is a mighty savior.
He will take delight in you with gladness.
With his love, he will calm all your fears.
He will rejoice over you with joyful songs (Zephaniah 3:17 NLT).

Your Father takes great delight in you. He doesn't merely tolerate you—He rejoices in you. He throws a great celebration when you join His family. He will correct you when you do wrong, but that is so you will become more like Him.

For God made Christ, who never sinned, to be the offering for our sin, so that we could be made right with God through Christ (2 Corinthians 5:21 NLT).

Jesus made you right with God. You did nothing to earn what Jesus did for you. You take on His goodness and righteousness because He died for you, and you are now in right standing with your Creator. You can approach God without fear, and you can also bring others to Him as His ambassador. God gives you the power to live right and invite others to become right with Him.

———————

Make allowance for each other's faults, and forgive anyone who offends you. Remember, the Lord forgave you, so you must forgive others (Colossians 3:13 NLT).

God has forgiven you. You are His son, and He does not hold your past sins against you. Since you have been forgiven, you have the power and responsibility to forgive others. If God has given grace to you, then He expects you to extend His grace to others.

———————

For we are God's masterpiece. He has created us anew in Christ Jesus, so we can do the good things he planned for us long ago (Ephesians 2:10 NLT).

You are not here by accident; God created you for a great purpose. He had plans for your life even before you were in your mother's womb. Your first responsibility is to know God and give glory to Him. Jesus has delivered you from sin through His sacrifice. As a son of God, you can walk with confidence and authority because you belong to Him.

———————

This means that anyone who belongs to Christ has become a new person. The old life is gone; a new life has begun! (2 Corinthians 5:17 NLT).

God has made you a new creation in Jesus Christ. All the old ways of defining yourself are now gone. Your way of seeing the world is forever changed. You are God's friend, and He is yours. He knows you as a beloved son, not as a slave, sinner, or enemy. Jesus paid for your sin in full, and He restored you to your Creator.

The Problem with Evolution

The Bible's grand story tells us we were created in the image of God, Christ died for us individually and collectively, and when we die, we have an eternal destiny based on our free will response to God. On the other hand, evolution says we were created in the image of the last organism from which we evolved, sin is a social construct from which we need no redemption, and when we die, we simply cease to exist. In summary, evolutionary theory strips us of our God-given identity.

The psalmist writes,

> For You formed my inward parts;
> You covered me in my mother's womb.
> I will praise You, for I am fearfully *and* wonderfully made;
> Marvelous are Your works,
> And *that* my soul knows very well.
> My frame was not hidden from You,
> When I was made in secret,
> *And* skillfully wrought in the lowest parts of the earth.
> Your eyes saw my substance, being yet unformed.
> And in Your book they all were written,
> The days fashioned for me,
> When *as yet there were* none of them.
> How precious also are Your thoughts to me, O God!
> How great is the sum of them!
> *If* I should count them, they would be more in number than the sand;
> When I awake, I am still with You (Psalm 139:13–18).

America has been raising an entire generation to believe they are no better than animals. In fact, Christians have been accused by radical animal rights activists of being *speciesists*. If you aren't familiar with that term, *speciesism* is "the human-held belief that all other animal species are inferior."[3] It is considered to be discrimination against animals, similar to how racism is discrimination against a particular race. Now, we condemn the mistreatment and abuse of animals. All animals are God's creation, and they should be treated as such. However, they are not His most precious creation. Humans and animals are not equals. In Luke 12:7, Jesus said, "The very hairs on your head are all numbered. So don't be afraid; you are more valuable to God than a whole flock of sparrows" (NLT).

In the grand picture of evolution, you are no more important than rats or cockroaches, but according to the Bible, you are divinely made. You are beloved. You are special. You have more value than you will ever understand. The enemy wants to strip us down and beat us up until we have no self-esteem; he wants to tell us we're animals so we will act like animals. But Jesus wants us to believe we are sons of the living God and act like it!

Knowing who you are in Christ gives you an unshakable identity. You become a more confident person, and you are better equipped as a parent to protect and defend your children. Ever since the Garden of Eden, Satan has been an identity thief, and the battle for identity will continue until we see the Lord face to face. But as we look forward to that day, we can fight victoriously as we believe and declare the truth of God's Word over ourselves and our families.

Knowing who you are in Christ gives you an unshakable identity.

11

United We Stand

Throughout our decades of ministry, we have heard many parents make statements like this one: "We're too busy with the kids to work on our marriage right now, but when they're gone, it will change." What a sad thing to say! While it's true that the kids will most likely leave when they reach adulthood, they will be leaving without the benefit of seeing what a healthy marriage looks like. Plus, the parents will have years of resentment, frustration, and disappointment to deal with—and that's *if* they're willing to put in effort to save their dying relationship. Wouldn't it be better for everyone to do the work now?

We realize that some people reading this book are single parents. If that's you, then please know that we love you so much, and we never want you to feel left out or ostracized. The reason we are including a chapter about marriage in a parenting book is not only to encourage married parents but also to help single parents prepare for marriage in the future. If you have any desire to be married someday, now is a great time to learn everything you can in order to be the best parent *and* the best spouse you can be.

You don't have to have the perfect relationship in order to be successful in marriage and parenting, but you do need to close ranks. Originally a military phrase, to close ranks means "to unite in a concerted stand, especially to meet a challenge."[1] Imagine you and your spouse are guards trying to protect your family from intruders. The bigger the gap between the two of you, the easier it is for intruders to slip past you. But when you close ranks, you stand shoulder to shoulder or, even better, face to face. Nothing can come between you, and you are offensively *and* defensively stronger.

In Mark 3:25, Jesus says, "If a house is divided against itself, that house cannot stand." Some of the best dividers are children. They are master manipulators (it's almost as though they go to school for it!), and as soon as they divide the parents, it's game, set, and match. Divided parents cannot succeed in parenting. You and your spouse must be a united front.

Here are some ways to build unity in your relationship:

Be a Two-Headed Monster

When your child wants something, which parent do they ask? When your child gets in trouble, which parent do they confide in? Children always know who has the open wallet, who will say yes, and who is the soft one. And they will play mom and dad off each other.

You and your spouse won't always agree on everything, but you can decide not to disagree in front of the kids. Dad can't say one thing while Mom says another. The mantra of parenting needs to be, "Let me talk to your mom. Let me talk to your dad." Your children need to know that you and your spouse are a two-headed monster that cannot be divided. They can't talk to one head without talking to the other.

Here's an example of how that conversation would go:

Child: "Can I go to the movies with my friends?"

Dad: "Let me talk to your mother."

Child: "Oh, she won't mind."

Dad: "I want to hear it from her lips."

Now, if it's a simple decision, it's fine to make it alone, but parenting often isn't simple. If your children catch even a hint of disagreement, they will put you on the spot. Don't let your kids play you against your spouse. Never say things like, "I'd let you go, but your mother won't," or "It's fine with me, but your dad says no." That creates a good cop, bad cop situation that brings confusion and division into the family.

In order to be a successful two-headed monster, you and your spouse need to figure out what you believe. What are the core values that form the foundation of your family? What are the second-tier issues on which you can compromise? But remember—no compromising in front of the children. Never argue about them in front of them. As far as the children know, you are a united front. You both show them the same amount of affection and concern, and you both discipline the same way.

In order to be a successful two-headed monster, you and your spouse need to figure out what you believe.

After our children were in bed, Jimmy and I (Karen) would go in our room and have parenting "discussions." Brent and I had very similar personalities, so it was easy for me to understand him. Jimmy and Julie have very similar personalities, so it was easy for him to understand her. But I had a difficult time understanding Julie, and Jimmy had a difficult time understanding Brent. So we would sit down and represent the kids to each other, always knowing that our marriage was more important than our children. Jimmy would say, "Karen, you don't understand what Julie is saying." I would reply, "Oh, I know *exactly* what she's saying. I'm a woman, and you aren't." He would respond, "No, what she really means is ..." And we would sit there and help each other understand the kids.

At the end of the conversations, we would say, "This is what we are going to do." In the morning, our children didn't know anything about these conversations. All they knew was that we were a two-headed monster, and we could not be divided.

Teach Honor and Respect

Always honor each other in front of your children. If you have something you need to say to your spouse, say it behind closed doors. Don't ever disrespect each other or be sarcastic and demeaning. Your children will pick up on it immediately, and they will do the same thing.

Always make your children honor your spouse. If I (Jimmy) ever heard Brent or Julie disrespect Karen, I never made Karen defend herself. I walked straight into the room and said, "Don't talk to your mother that way. Apologize to her right now." Unity means what the kids do to one parent is what they do to both parents. If you pick a fight with Mom, then you've got a fight with Dad. And Karen honored me in the same way.

When I speak at marriage conferences, I often jokingly tell parents that children only want one thing: to possess your soul! Children want 100 percent, 24/7 access to their parents, and they do not recognize boundaries unless they are taught to do so.

If you don't teach your children to respect your marriage, you won't have one. Your kids will consume your every waking moment, leaving you too exhausted and intruded upon to prioritize your marriage. You will always love your children, but raising them is a temporary assignment. Someday they will grow up, move out, and start families of their own. (That's the goal, anyway.) Your children need to understand that they do not have unlimited access to you. You have a marriage and a relationship with God that come before they do.

We (Jimmy and Karen) raised our children to respect our marriage, and we modeled the way they should love their spouses one day. When Brent and Julie were young, we would eat dinner as a family and spend time together. We then put the kids to bed around 8 pm and allowed them to read books until they went to sleep. We told them that as soon as they were in bed, it was Mom and Dad's time to be together, and they were not allowed to cross the threshold of their room unless it was an emergency. Of course, they tried to come out for various reasons, but we reminded them, "We had our time with you, and now we're having our time with each other."

We had a little sitting area in our bedroom, and we would sit face to face and talk. And naturally we would be sexually intimate at times. One night, Julie picked our *locked* door, and walked in on us while we were having sex. Needless to say, it was a shocking moment for all of us, and she never did that again!

Create Disciplines and Traditions

A successful marriage is not about what you can make happen once. The three of us could probably do a backflip one time (after which you'd have to visit us in the hospital), but we couldn't keep doing it. If your marriage is in trouble, the goal is to find out how to get it back on track and *keep* it on track. This requires creating new disciplines and traditions to redirect your time and energy to your spouse in a prioritized, regular manner. Even if the passion in your marriage has faded because of the problems that have existed, you can still make your relationship a priority.

A successful marriage is not about what you can make happen once.

Do you have a date night every week where you can pursue each other? Do you take trips? We (Jimmy and Karen) used to take a trip every six or seven weeks for just a night or two, leaving our kids with the grandparents. Now, before you object that you don't have enough money, let us explain that we were broke. Our funds were extremely limited, and the hotels we stayed at could best be described as "cheap" or "crummy." But you know what? We loved it. We always looked forward to our time away together.

Not everyone understands the importance of time alone together, because not everyone understands the law of priority. When my two girls were growing up, I (Julie) had a regular weekly date night with my husband Cory, and everyone in our family loved it. The girls got fun time away from Mom and Dad, and Cory and I got that much-needed quality time together. But one day I found out that some women in my friend group were making fun of me. Worse yet, they were labeling me as a bad mom for not putting my kids first. I had to make a decision right then and there that I was going to be faithful to God's Word. And you know what? Years later, those same moms came up to me and apologized. They saw how strong my marriage was because of the intentional time Cory and I poured into it, and they realized that our girls were actually better off and more well-adjusted because of it.

Here are some good disciplines and traditions to build into your marriage to keep you close and ensure that both of your needs are met in a prioritized and energetic manner:

- A weekly date night
- Praying together and going to church
- Taking walks together
- Taking short, overnight, or weekend trips
- Talking face-to-face without distractions every day
- Planning times to have sex when you are both rested
- Not going to bed angry (talking things out and forgiving each other)
- Reading a marriage book together
- Going to a marriage conference

- Watching a romantic comedy together
- Finding something you both enjoy doing and doing it regularly

Remember, when you are practicing your new lifestyle, you are teaching your children to respect your marriage and training them for a successful future.

Get Outside Help

When your child sees that you are happy and secure, it makes them happy and secure. Why? Because children see and internalize everything. Even if you and your spouse are not fighting in front of them, your child can sense any tension in your relationship, and they will internalize it. Happiness and security in a marriage are essential for raising healthy, responsible children.

If you and your spouse are having a long-term struggle and have reached an impasse, go outside your marriage for counseling and input. Now, let's be clear: this does *not* mean posting about your problems on social media or griping about your spouse on a group text to all your friends. Both of those tactics will only serve to hurt your relationship. Instead, find a biblically sound, trustworthy authority figure who will help you navigate the issue.

We (Jimmy and Karen) found ourselves with a circumstance that we couldn't solve by talking it out, and it went on for a while. It was a disagreement about one of our kids, and it was coming up every day in our family. I (Jimmy) had my opinion, and Karen had her opinion, and we just couldn't get on the same page. I told Karen, "Pick someone for us to go talk to, and I'll submit to whatever they say." So we went to see a counselor we both respect, and when we got to her office, I said, "We are not here just to get your advice. We are here to submit to your counsel. We have an impasse in our family, and there's something going on with one of our children that we cannot solve. We're going to tell you what's happening, and whatever you say is going to be God's voice to us. We've already decided that." So she asked what was happening, and we both gave our sides. The counselor looked at me and said, "Jimmy, you're wrong," and she explained to me the reason why. And she was right. I just hadn't been able to see it because I was too opinionated and too emotionally involved. You see, that counselor may have seemed like she was taking Karen's side, but it was actually God's side.

When you reach an impasse, don't let it destroy your marriage. Don't let it take you out. Everyone comes to these times in their marriage and in their parenting where they can't solve problems on their own. Getting help is not a sign of weakness; it's a sign of wisdom. Wise people get help. Rich people have financial counselors all around them. It's the people going broke who aren't reading books on money. People who want to be successful parents read books, go to seminars, and learn all they can about parenting. We have seen far too many parents whose kids are falling apart, and they won't ask for help or take any advice. You must have a teachable spirit. That's part of the mindset of success.

Getting help is not a sign of weakness; it's a sign of wisdom.

Have Faith

Parenting takes faith, especially in the days in which we are living now. You're not a bad parent because your child pushes every boundary and parameter. You're just a parent! And once you master one age, your child will move on to the next. It's constantly challenging. Someone once told us, "You never know if you're a success until your child turns 30." We aren't sure if we entirely agree with that age, but this is what we saw in Julie and Brent.

Julie was always a good girl, but she was *very* strong-willed. When she left home, we saw a dramatic increase in maturity in the years right after she went to college. A little later, Brent went to Baylor University, and he definitely tested his boundaries. We had some very intense "fellowship" over his lifestyle, and we even threatened to defund his life if he kept it up. Brent called me (Jimmy) one day and said, "I want to come home and be accountable to you and Mom." I was shocked. He came home and still tested some boundaries until he asked Stephanie (his future wife) out on a date. She turned him down, saying, "I'm not dating you. You don't live for God." Brent told me that Stephanie had turned him down because he wasn't living for God, and he wanted to know what I thought about it. I responded, "That's the girl we've been praying for." Then I asked, "Do you want to go out with her bad enough to live for God?" Brent did, so he repented and changed his life. He is a man of God to this day, and he and Stephanie have now been married for more than 25 years.

———————

Your children will grow up and leave home one day. What kind of marriage will you be left with—cold and distant or intimate and fulfilling? And what model for marriage will you have given them as they begin their new lives? No family is perfect, and it is not our intention to bring any shame or condemnation on you if you have experienced the pain of divorce. We all have some degree of dysfunction, and it is only with God's help that we can learn and grow as we seek His will for our lives.

12

Joining Ranks

In a traditional nuclear family, two people get married, and then children come around that marriage. The marriage serves as a nucleus for the family. A family built around children, or anything else, would be like an atom without a nucleus. Without a nucleus, the atomic particles—the protons, neutrons, and electrons—have nothing to orbit around.

In a blended family relationship, one or both parents have children first, and then there is a marriage. According to the United States Census Bureau, "over 50 percent of US families are remarried or re-coupled" and "1300 new stepfamilies are forming every day."[1] Because the children existed before the relationship did, it's very tempting for the family to orbit around them. But that's not the way God designed the family. Regardless of what came first, marriage must be the center of the family. Only then can every person in the family find true happiness.

Regardless of what came first, marriage must be the center of the family.

If you are part of a blended family, then you know you are facing some unique challenges. Divorce rates are higher in second, third, and subsequent marriages. But here's some good news: if you commit yourself to God's design for marriage and family, you have every chance of success. You can fight for your family!

The Law of Priority

In the law of priority, God comes first, your spouse comes second, and your children come third. While this can be difficult for traditional families, it can be even trickier for blended (nontraditional) families. How can you put someone first who has only been in your life for a short time when you have children that you've known and loved from the moment they were born?

I (Jimmy) have counseled many people who said, "My children are permanent, but my new spouse may not be." The problem with that kind of thinking is that the parent is giving more regard—more value or "weight"—to the children than the new spouse in every decision. This is especially common in times of serious conflict. The mindset is, *If this marriage doesn't last, I don't want my children to resent me for the rest of my life for choosing my new spouse over them. So I'll consider the possibility of divorce in this decision as I prefer my children over my new spouse.*

A standard like that—controlled by fear—will only create a downward spiral of bad decisions, leading to bad feelings in the marriage, leading to the parent's fears coming true. If you see yourself in this downward cycle, stop letting fear control you. Take control of your thoughts and let common sense and wisdom lead you.

Consider this:

- Your children are only in your home for about 18 or so years, but your marriage is for a lifetime.

- Your children cannot be equipped for success in their marriages and families if you don't provide a good example for them. They need to see you building a good marriage and working through your problems.

The security and happiness of your children depends a great deal on the stability of your marriage, so don't fear their response or let them control you. Just do the right thing and believe God for the right results. By the way, if a bad marriage scarred your children, a good marriage can heal them.

If you truly want to succeed in your marriage, then make your marriage your priority. Let your spouse and your children know through your actions, words, and attitudes that you are committed to your marriage, and that it is your highest priority. All successful families with married couples in them are built around the marriage, not the children.

The Law of Partnership

Like the law of priority, there is another law that must be obeyed for a marriage to be successful. This is the *law of partnership*. Genesis 2:24 says, "This explains why a man leaves his father and mother and is joined to his wife, and the two are united into one" (NLT). God designed marriage to operate as a complete joining and sharing of two lives. The intimacy and union of marriage is so profound that God used the word "one" to describe it.

How do two things become one? They meld. Everything that was owned or administrated separately is now surrendered to the co-ownership and control of the relationship. We realize this can be a very touchy subject, and many parents who remarry try to treat their children as an exception to this rule. Because the children have been through a lot, the biological parent will often try to protect them from further hurt. That usually means not allowing the new spouse to give input or have influence regarding their kids. They refuse to share ownership.

Now, we are *not* saying a new spouse should replace the other biological parent. Not at all. But we *are* saying the new spouse must be an equal parent. Marriage is about trust. If you don't trust a person with your children, you should never marry them. That would be a huge mistake. When you marry someone, they become co-owners of everything in your life.

When you marry someone, they become co-owners of everything in your life.

One common objection we've heard is, "My new spouse doesn't love my children like I do!" Let's talk about that for a moment. Certainly, your spouse may not love your children like you do. There's a biological bond in place that is one of the strongest forces in the universe. But thinking like that only perpetuates the fear that your spouse will not make the right decisions related to your children because he or she is not motivated by the same level of compassion and concern.

The greatest love on earth is a decision, not an emotion. Jesus said, "Love your neighbor as yourself" (Matthew 22:39 NLT). The word Jesus uses for love is *agape*, which we already talked about, and it means love by choice. Just as God chooses to love us, your spouse can choose to love your children as much as you do, and you can choose to love their children as much as they do. Love doesn't require genetics—it just requires choice.

Children are loyal to their biological parents, and they naturally want their biological parents to be together. It's very common for a child to resent a new stepparent. One man that I (Jimmy) know really well married a woman who already had teenage boys. At the wedding, one of the sons came up to him and said, "I'm going to make your life miserable." This child was resentful of the fact that his parents had divorced and his mom had remarried, and he and his brothers absolutely tormented their new stepdad. The stepdad was powerless because his wife wouldn't let him have any authority over "her" children. This was a good man, by the way—he never would have abused those children. But he wasn't even allowed to correct them or defend himself. Anytime he brought it up to his wife, she would say, "If you're asking me to choose between you and my children, I choose my children." So what do you think happened? They divorced. It was an unlivable situation.

If you think you're doing your children a favor by withholding them from your new marriage to protect them, you're wrong. It only perpetuates insecurity within them as it allows them to divide you from your spouse and sabotage your new marriage. This is where you need to lose the word "my" and adopt the word "ours"— whether it's with children, money, or anything else.

Now, when it comes to discipline, it's usually better if the biological parent enforces the discipline on their biological children, especially when the marriage is new and the relationship between the children and the new spouse is still developing. But even then, the new spouse must be allowed to have input. You must be a team and be influenced by each other. Anything you refuse to surrender to your spouse will damage your relationship and create deep resentment.

A healthy blended family says, "We love our children. Even though I'm not your biological parent, every decision that we make will be made together. Regardless of biological or non-biological child, we will not be divided in our parenting. They are all *our* children, and all decisions will be made together."

When you make a decision together, there can't be a preference for your biological children or their biological children. There can't be things you do for one child that you don't do for another child. In every family, fairness is important, but in blended families, it's extremely important.

We will say it again: if you don't trust a person with your children, then don't marry them! Marriage is trust, and the children need to see both spouses operating as a parenting team. You can do that in ways that will not make your children feel rejected or cause them to resent your spouse. Simply let everyone know that you are there to stay, and your marriage will not be laid on the altar of your children's opinions, emotions, or reactions.

Now that we have established the proper foundation, let's look at some unique issues in blended families.

Modesty

In a biological family, parents rarely view their children as sex objects, and biological siblings are rarely attracted to each other sexually. But in a non-biological family, these natural barriers aren't present. This doesn't mean there needs to be an atmosphere of mistrust—again, marriage requires trust—but it is wise to have higher standards of modesty. No one should be walking around naked or in their underwear. Every family member should use common sense when it comes to decency and propriety, especially when being around the opposite sex.

Accountability

One of our relatives married into a blended family situation. Her new spouse was a good man who paid his ex-wife child support in order to provide for their children. But every time he wrote the check, our relative got more and more upset. She just couldn't handle the fact that this money was going to his ex-wife, and it tormented her.

The law of partnership says, "Your debts are my debts. Your assets are my assets. Your liabilities are my liabilities. If you have children from a previous marriage that need to be supported, I fully own that, and I will fully support you and your children with a good attitude." Sadly, our relative didn't do that, and her marriage imploded.

Visitation

One of the most agonizing issues we have ever helped families with is visitation. We have seen everything from the most bizarre displays of an unhealthy ex-spouse spoiling children to indoctrinating the children against their other biological parent and their beliefs.

I (Jimmy) can remember one particular family, in which an ex-spouse was spoiling the children and letting them have all kinds of exposure to ungodliness whenever they visited him and his new wife. Every time the children went to their home, they were fed all kinds of nonsense and allowed to watch terrible things.

The mom was very concerned, but legally, there wasn't anything she could do. It isn't against the law to play your children against your ex-spouse and spoil them so they will like you more. She came to me and said, "Jimmy, what do I do?" My response was this:

Number one: do not communicate through the children. Communicate directly with your ex-spouse and their spouse, and don't use those children as messengers.

Number two: every time those children leave your home, pray over those kids. Pray protection over their minds, their hearts, their memories, their sexuality, their attitudes, etc. Pray that God will go with them wherever they go and supernaturally protect them.

Number three: do not take for granted every day you have with that child. Don't play the enemy's game. Be righteous. Love those children. Take them to church. Be fun and be fair. Do not underestimate the power of God to impact their hearts. Righteousness is more powerful than sin. The Spirit of God is more powerful than the spirit of the devil. And don't let fear and discouragement get over you. Pray over your children coming and going.

When those children mature, they'll bless you for your righteousness.

And don't lower your standards because somebody else has. They'll lose that fight, I promise you. When those children mature, they'll bless you for your righteousness.

Scott and Vanessa Martindale are the founders of Blended Kingdom Families, an incredible ministry that we are proud to partner with at XO Marriage. The mission of Blended Kingdom Families is to break the generational cycle of divorce, equip marriages, and unite blended families with the truth of God's Word. Scott and Vanessa know firsthand the incredible amount of faith it takes to be a blended family living God's way, and they share their passion and wisdom on their *Blended Kingdom Families* podcast and in their book *Blended and Redeemed: The Go-to Field Guide for the Modern Stepfamily*. (There's a study guide and a pastor's guide too!)

In *Blended and Redeemed*, Scott and Vanessa share how the battle for the family is a spiritual battle:

> The breakdown of society begins with the breakdown of the family unit. If the enemy can get to our children, he can destroy our legacies. If he destroys our legacies, then he controls the world. The book of Genesis says that the seed of man will crush the head of the enemy (see Genesis 3:15). Our children, our *legacy*, are key to that promise, so our legacy is the natural enemy of the serpent. Therefore, he will never stop trying to kill it. It is an act of self-preservation for him.
>
> Kingdom legacy is all about breaking generational curses. It's about teaching and training our children in the Word. It's about showing our children what godly, healthy marriages look like. It's loving others as Christ loves us. It's living a life of forgiveness. It's embracing restoration. It's accepting our position as a new creation in Christ. It's remembering that we are who we are *right now*, not who we were *back then*. Legacy is, in effect, a generational game-changer.[2]

Scott and Vanessa understand that fighting for your blended family takes courage, patience, and perseverance. But you don't have to do it alone.

The mission verse for our Blended Kingdom Families ministry is Luke 1:37: "For nothing will be impossible with God." God gave us that verse at the outset of the ministry because He knew this blended family life would often *seem* impossible. You most likely know that already. Most blended families we know have already walked through the fire or are in the midst of it. But there's good news: *God is fireproof.* He'll walk with you through the most intense heat and deliver you safely out the other side.[3]

13

Be the First

When fighting a war, one of the hardest places to be is on the front lines. You are the first to engage with the enemy and the first to discover what battle strategies don't work. At times, it can be scary or even disheartening, but you know you can't give up for the sake of the soldiers coming after you.

The same concept is true for parenting. You may be the first generation in your family to raise your children according to biblical principles. As you look at your family tree, there might not be any godly examples of success for you to follow, and instead, you have to deal with all the baggage that came from their failed attempts. This doesn't mean you don't love or respect your family. Rather, you recognize that there are things you need to recover from in order to pass a different inheritance onto your children.

Family History

We (Jimmy and Karen) should not have had to spend our twenties getting over our childhoods, but we did. Now, our parents weren't bad people; actually, they were better than they should have been, given their own very dysfunctional childhoods. We're going to share a little bit of their histories with you now.

My (Jimmy's) maternal grandfather started drinking whiskey and smoking cigarettes when he was five years old. He was a very sweet man when sober but very mean when drunk. His daughter (my mother) was very beautiful, and she was voted homecoming queen, prettiest girl in school, etc. Well, when he got drunk, my grandfather would find my mother and publicly shame and humiliate her.

As I shared in the first section, my father was one of 10 children in an incredibly poor family. He grew up to be a salesman who worked all the time, and whenever he came home, he would sit in a chair and essentially ignore us. My dad opened his own appliance and electronics store, and after college, I went to work for him for seven years. He was a really good boss to work for because that was his world, and he talked more to me at work than he ever had at home.

Then the church Karen and I were attending asked me to come on staff as a marriage counselor. I agreed, and when the senior pastor left 10 months later, I became the senior pastor of the church. I pastored there for 30 years. But when I told my dad that the church had offered me a job, he told me, "Jimmy, the only thing that church needs is your money. You sit right here and make a lot of money in this business, and you give them your money. That's all they need from you." I said, "Daddy, I'm sorry. The Lord has called me into the ministry, and even though I love working for you, I'm going to go to work for the church." Well, my dad didn't take it well. In fact, he said, "I never want to see you again. Get out!" That day, my family disowned me.

I (Karen) don't have a much better story. My mom was in a farming accident when she was 14, and she lost an arm and a leg. Somehow, she raised three children with one arm and one leg, and while she is a remarkable person, she brought horrific scars from her childhood into her marriage and parenting.

My dad was raised by a very vulgar and abusive father who was much older than him (and much older than my grandmother), and like my mother, my dad was very scarred from his childhood. Together, they used domination and shame to control my siblings and me. They would yell at us and belittle us and put us down constantly.

I grew up with an immense amount of shame, and it bled into every area of my life, especially as a young wife and mother. When Julie was a baby, she was very moody and often had a scowl on her face. One day, my parents took me aside and asked what was wrong with her. My maternal instinct wanted to say "Nothing! That's my baby!" but I didn't have the courage to stand up to them. And I had a similar reaction when the wife of one of our church elders judged me for wearing a nice fur coat. My dad had given it to me as a gift for Christmas, and I had been afraid to wear it because I didn't want people to think Jimmy and I were frivolous or prideful. Finally, my friends convinced me that I should just enjoy the coat, so I wore it. Then this elder's wife, who already didn't like our family, came up to me and said, "How dare you wear that coat! Who do you think you are?" I realize that most people wouldn't have cared what she thought, but because shame was such a part of me, I cared *so much*.

Even though my family was a bit more "high society" than Jimmy's family, we came from the exact same value system. Our families valued three things and in this order:

1. Money

2. Social status

3. Family

Our parents thought if they had money and social status, they could give their children everything they needed. While these values are common, they created horrific pain for another generation.

One example is my (Karen's) brother, who is several years younger than me. Growing up, he hated our dad so much that he did everything he could to punish him for his parenting failures. Now, our parents eventually got saved, and for 40-plus years, our dad tried to mend that broken relationship. Still, when Dad died in 2020, my brother refused to come to his funeral. He lives on the other side of the world, and he has nothing to do with our family to this day. While I don't excuse his behavior, I do understand that it is based in the pain of our broken family value system.

A New Value System

Every parent needs to think about the generational effects of their behavior. A godly parent wants to create a life that gives their children every advantage going forward. In other words, they want God's generational blessing on their family. You cannot have the mentality that the only thing that matters is you in the here and now.

Every parent needs to think about the generational effects of their behavior.

As young parents, we (Jimmy and Karen) sat down one day and decided we didn't want to raise our children the way we were raised. We didn't want our children to spend their twenties and thirties recovering from us. We wanted to build our family right, and so here was our value system:

1. God

2. Family

3. Everything else

We have absolutely no regrets. Our children and grandchildren all serve the Lord, and we have a wonderful family.

Now, we aren't saying that we were perfect or that our children didn't have to deal with issues related to us. But we are watching the blessing of our children to the third and fourth generation, and we know that's what every parent wants. Your value system is how you're going to get that.

Your children need two things: God and you. Even if you don't have that much money—even if you can't afford the latest expensive sneakers—if your children have you and God, then they are rich. That's the truth.

Parenting on the Rock

> Therefore whoever hears these sayings of Mine, and does them, I will liken him to a wise man who built his house on the rock: and the rain descended, the floods came, and the winds blew and beat on that house; and it did not fall, for it was founded on the rock.
>
> But everyone who hears these sayings of Mine, and does not do them, will be like a foolish man who built his house on the sand: and the rain descended, the floods came, and the winds blew and beat on that house; and it fell. And great was its fall (Matthew 7:24–27).

I (Jimmy) read this passage in my early twenties, and I wondered, *Why would anyone build on the sand instead of the rock?* Perhaps you've wondered that too. Well, for starters, sand is more popular. When you go to the beach, you see people lying on the sand, not the rocks. But why? Because sand is more comfortable and more conformable. When you get up after lying on sand, it looks like you. You've left your imprint in it. But when you lie on a rock, it leaves its imprint in you. Jesus is the Rock, and He isn't going to conform to whatever shape we want Him to be. Rather, we conform to Him. He is the Son of God, and we are His disciples.

We aren't living in a non-biblical culture—we're living in an *anti*-biblical culture with a custom-made Christianity. The attitude of many people is "Take what you want from the Bible and leave what you don't want" and "I'm a Christian in spite of my sinful lifestyle." That's not what Jesus is about, though. We either accept Him for who He is, or we reject Him. Those are the only two options.

If you're living on the Rock, Jesus offers two promises:

1. You will be persecuted by the world.
2. You will have total security.

When the storms of life hit, the Rock is the most peaceful place on earth. Your family isn't hurt, your marriage lasts, your children survive, your finances succeed, and everything is blessed. You might lose friends who prefer the sand, but in the long run, the Rock is the only place to build your life.

Psalm 119:105 says, "Your word is a lamp to my feet / And a light to my path." When you build your life on the Word, you are invincible. The devil can't beat you! You don't have to be afraid of the devil, but he should definitely be afraid of you.

Many people who build their lives on the sand believe what the Bible says—they just don't do it. "I can't forgive because it's too hard." But part of being a Christian is doing hard things that other people don't do. Don't you think it was hard for Jesus to look down from the cross and forgive the people who put Him there? Of course! No one has done anything to us that is even close to what they did to Jesus. If Jesus can forgive the people who crucified Him, we can forgive the people who have hurt us.

When you have a rock beneath you, it can be hard and uncomfortable. But when the bad times come, you will thank God that something hard is underneath you. Peace comes from successful spiritual warfare and building your life on the Word of God. When the Bible is your foundation, then your life is peaceful, even while everyone else's is falling apart. Everyone else may be losing, but you are gaining.

We (Jimmy and Karen) decided when our children were young that we were going to raise our kids according to the Bible to the best of our ability. But some friends of ours read a parenting book by a popular psychiatrist and decided that his way was the right way, even though it went entirely against what the Bible says about raising children. Years later, when all our children were in their late teens, the psychiatrist was proven to be a fraud. His own children said he was the worst father you could possibly imagine, and everyone in his family was scarred because of him. Imagine the regrets our friends had for all the years wasted on instilling the faulty values of this "expert"!

If you raise your children on the Word of God, you will have no regrets. The Word of God is the same yesterday, today, and forever, and God will never change his mind. It is an unchangeable, stable foundation.

If you raise your children on the Word of God, you will have no regrets.

There are going to be storms; the foundation of your life is going to be tested. But if you build your life upon the Word of God, you, your children, and your grandchildren will be standing when other people are falling.

———

When I (Jimmy) became a senior pastor, my parents thought I was crazy. (Even worse, they thought our church was a cult, which made me the cult leader.) They disowned me and didn't speak to me for ten months. But several years later my parents went through a very significant tragedy, and they called me. I went over and sat down with them, and I could see that they were broken. They said, "We don't know what to do." I said, "You made your business your god. Your entire universe was that business, and that's why God wouldn't bless it. You need the Lord." My parents both got saved that day.

I said, "I want to see you in church on Sunday." My parents had never been in church my entire life, but that Sunday, they were in the back row. People kept coming up and hugging them, which was surprising for my parents because they were not touchy, physically affectionate people. After church, my parents asked me, "Why are they coming up hugging us like that? Do those people know us?" I said, "They just love you." My parents couldn't understand because they had only ever known love for two reasons: money and social status. That's the curse when you're living for the world. But as Christians, we have love because of Jesus Christ. It's a totally different value system.

My parents became the first people to arrive every Sunday, and they were the last people to leave. They stood at the back door and met everybody that came in and hugged them. There's something about affection from a Christian that heals a heart. It healed my parents.

Before he passed away, my dad told me a thousand times how proud he was of me. He loved to tell me, "You're a better preacher than Billy Graham." We were eating lunch one day, and my parents said, "Thank you for not raising our grandchildren the way we raised you." I had been disowned, but I saw the healing of my family.

Some of you were raised in generations of a Christian family, so you really can't relate to our stories in this chapter. But some of you came out of brokenness the way we did. You may be the first Christian in your family. You may be the first couple in your family willing to take a stand for God. Being the first takes courage, but it is the best thing you will ever do—both for yourself and for your entire family.

14

Gatekeeper

Personal Gates

In Matthew chapter 16, Jesus mentions the church for the first time: "You are Peter, a stone; and upon this rock I will build my church; and all the powers of hell shall not prevail against it. And I will give you the keys of the Kingdom of Heaven; whatever doors you lock on earth shall be locked in heaven; and whatever doors you open on earth shall be open in heaven!" (vv. 18–19 TLB). Jesus is responding to Peter's confession, "You are the Christ, the Son of the living God" (v. 16), and it's upon this confession that Jesus is going to build His church. Whatever Peter locks temporarily (on earth) will be locked eternally (in heaven), and whatever he unlocks temporarily will be unlocked eternally. Peter is, in essence, a gatekeeper.

Adam and Eve were the first gatekeepers of the earth, but when Satan came and knocked on the door of their lives through temptation, they allowed him to come in and wreak all kinds of havoc. That's why Jesus' words to Peter are so significant—the Lord is redelivering the keys of the earth to believers. Jesus gives us the keys to the entire kingdom of heaven, and whatever we want to lock and disallow on this earth, He stands behind us. Whatever we want to allow and to set free, Jesus stands behind us. We have total authority over all the power of the enemy, and he cannot harm us as long as we're using the keys Jesus has given us to lock and unlock.

We have total authority over all the power of the enemy

Satan has no authority to harm believers, but we have authority over him. You never have to fear the enemy—he fears you. Jesus said, "Behold, I give you the authority to trample on serpents and scorpions, and over all the power of the enemy, and nothing shall by any means hurt you" (Luke 10:19). If Satan could kill you, you'd already be dead. He hates you, and the fact that you're still breathing is just a testimony to the fact that he has zero legitimate authority over your life.

Personal Gates

We must understand that God has given us authority to live safely as His family, and He empowers us to be the gatekeepers of our own lives. There are seven gates to your life that God or the enemy will use to do good or bad things in your life.

Eyes

> "The lamp of the body is the eye. If therefore your eye is good, your whole body will be full of light. But if your eye is bad, your whole body will be full of darkness. If therefore the light that is in you is darkness, how great *is* that darkness!" (Matthew 6:22–23).

- What articles, magazines, and books do you read?
- What TV shows and movies do you watch?
- What images do you look at on the internet?

Ears

"Pay close attention to what you hear. The closer you listen, the more understanding you will be given—and you will receive even more" (Mark 4:24 NLT).

- What music do you listen to?
- What podcasts do you subscribe to?
- What language do your friends, family members, and coworkers use around you?

Mouth

"Death and life *are* in the power of the tongue, / And those who love it will eat its fruit" (Proverbs 18:21).

- What words do you speak over yourself and others?
- How do you respond to rumors and gossip?
- How often do you worship and pray?

Mind

"For the weapons of our warfare *are* not carnal but mighty in God for pulling down strongholds, casting down arguments and every high thing that exalts itself against the knowledge of God, bringing every thought into captivity to the obedience of Christ" (2 Corinthians 10:4–5).

- What do you allow yourself to daydream about?
- What thoughts or ideas do you concentrate on?
- What beliefs do you actively try to build up or tear down?

Spirit

"Behold, I stand at the door and knock. If anyone hears My voice and opens the door, I will come in to him and dine with him, and he with Me" (Revelation 3:20).

- Do you live in rebellion and unbelief?
- Have you received salvation by grace through faith?
- Is Jesus the Lord and Savior of your life?

Flesh

"'For this reason a man shall leave his father and mother and be joined to his wife, and the two shall become one flesh'; so then they are no longer two, but one flesh. Therefore what God has joined together, let not man separate" (Mark 10:7–9).

- When you want something, who do you ask for help?
- What physical needs demand your attention?
- Who do you trust to meet your sexual desires?

Emotion

"For we do not have a High Priest who cannot sympathize with our weaknesses, but was in all *points* tempted as *we are, yet* without sin" (Hebrews 4:15).

- What are the biggest temptations you face?
- How do you respond when bad things happen?
- Do your feelings dictate your attitude?

You decide everything that comes into your life through these seven gates. Who you are today has been decided by you and what gate you opened. Your mom and dad didn't do it, and neither did

God. He doesn't decide how you feel, what you think, or where you put your eyes or your ears. And neither does Satan. We all are responsible for the gates of our lives. Everything in your life right now, you allowed to be there, and the things that are not in your life are not there because you disallowed them. Locking and unlocking made you who you are right now, for good or for bad.

We all are responsible for the gates of our lives.

Parenting Gates

Everything in your home, *you* allow. Everything not in your home, *you* disallow. God doesn't keep the gates of your home, and neither does the devil. Hopefully your children don't either. All the devil needs is a careless gatekeeper to corrupt a child's life.

Here are four gates of a child's life that a parent must diligently keep watch over:

God

God put His image on Adam and Eve in Genesis chapter 1 and then commanded them to multiply. They weren't ready to multiply until they bore the image of God. The number one responsibility you have as a parent is to lead your child to an understanding of the love and truth of God so that at the earliest age possible, he or she will accept Christ into his or her life. From that point forward, you are discipling them in their faith. Discipleship includes taking your child to church, reading the Bible to them, praying with them, etc. The God gate is the most important gate in your child's life.

And let us consider one another in order to stir up love and good works, not forsaking the assembling of ourselves together, *as* is the manner of some, but exhorting *one another*, and so much more as you see the Day approaching (Hebrews 10:24–25).

One of the most important things all three of us did as young parents was to decide that we would raise our kids in church. You need to have a group of people that you're with on a regular, committed basis that can encourage each other, hold each other accountable, and fight alongside each other. Your children will be like the people they surround themselves with, and we'll look at that more in the Friend Gate.

Friends

Your child's friends are their future. Let's read 1 Corinthians 15:33 again: "Do not be deceived: 'Bad company corrupts good morals'" (NASB). The Contemporary English Version says it even clearer: "Bad friends will destroy you."

You can never be too careful when it comes to your children, but you also can't be legalistic. Legalism always produces rebellion because it's based on rules and not relationship. You cannot march into your child's school and tell the teachers that your child is only allowed to hang out with the "good" kids. But you can train your child to know what signs to look for in a good friend. Encourage them to be the influencers, not the influenced. My (Julie's) daughters went to a public high school for their junior and senior years, and they had a very eclectic group of friends with various lifestyles and beliefs. They learned that they could love everyone while still standing up for their beliefs.

There may be times when your child needs to be removed from a situation, and God will give you wisdom to recognize those moments. But the key to most circumstances is open and honest communication. Tell your children, "We love you no matter what, and we only want the best for you. If you hear or see anything that goes against our family values, please tell us." Decide in advance that when your children tell you things, you won't have a big, emotional overreaction. Thank your children for trusting you and have a conversation—not a lecture—about what needs to happen in order to keep them safe.

Entertainment

In our society, many, if not most, children use some form of technology to access entertainment. A 2022 survey of American parents found that:

- 94 percent say their children under 13 use online apps (video streaming, video gaming, and show/movie streaming).
- 80 percent worry about their child's privacy when using those apps.
- 48 percent monitor their children's activity on apps daily.[1]

How can we say we are concerned about our children's privacy—their safety—and more than half of us aren't even aware of what they are doing every day? So many parents complain, "I'm just too busy to keep up with everything my kid does online." Obviously not everything on the internet is bad, but there is enough bad content on there to make the internet a very dangerous place for children who don't understand that there are things they should never see or hear. And when they do find these things, it's very tempting to keep coming back to them and to share them with friends.

Children are smarter than you think. I (Jimmy) was holding our two-year-old grandson Reid one day, and he said, "Pappy, I want to play on your phone." In less than 10 seconds, he had opened Netflix and was watching *Thomas the Tank Engine*. Now, this was okay because I was sitting right there with him, but what if he had accidentally pulled up an inappropriate show? And it's not just Netflix that parents need to be concerned about. There are apps specifically created to hide a person's activity on their electronic device, and they are designed to look very innocent (like a calculator, for example). If your child doesn't want you to see what they are doing on their phone or tablet, they simply download one of these apps and put all their pictures, videos, contacts, etc. inside it.

Yes, there are some great parent control programs designed to keep children safe online. We recommend doing your research to see what program is best and then installing it on every single device in your home. But even then, your children need supervision. You cannot give your child access to an electronic instrument that you are unwilling to monitor. Social media, video games, and YouTube are three huge categories of popular entertainment, and if you are going to allow your child to engage in them, then you must be willing to set and enforce age-appropriate boundaries. It's tempting to let entertainment raise your children, but you have to remember that as a parent, you are responsible for everything you allow into your home.

You cannot give your child access to an electronic instrument that you are unwilling to monitor.

(If you're not sure where or how to start, two fantastic resources are *TALK: A Practical Approach to Cyberparenting and Open Communication* and *Keeping Kids Safe in a Digital World: A Solution That Works.* The author of these two books is Christian mom and public speaker Mandy Majors. We'll talk more about her story later, but in her books, Mandy addresses everything from cell phones to social media to pornography, plus many other hot-button issues that parents simply can't afford to ignore.)

Education

Parents are responsible for educating their children. Let us say this another way: parents have the authority to educate their children. This doesn't mean you have to homeschool your child (unless that is what God tells you to do), but it does mean you are involved in your child's education. Children in the United States spend an average of 6.87 hours per day in school every Monday through Friday.[2] But what exactly are they learning? And who's in charge of making that decision?

The classroom has transitioned from a place of learning to a battleground for the identity of our children. Long gone are the times of beginning the school day with prayer and seeing the Ten Commandments posted on classroom walls. We live in a post-modern, post-Christian, and post-Bible culture, and there is a very real, targeted attack on biblical values in every part of our society, including the education sector.

As a Christian parent, a big part of fighting for your child's soul is being involved in their education, especially if they are part of the 90 percent of American students in public schools. You can't drop them off at the door and hope for the best. Your child needs you to know what they are learning, because it's not just reading, writing, and arithmetic anymore.

I (Karen) remember one day when Julie came home from her elementary school down the street and questioned a basic Christian belief. She looked at Jimmy and me and asked, "Why is that right? Just because *you* say it's right?" Now, we didn't have a problem with Julie asking a question about faith. We always encouraged both her and Brent to ask anything on their minds. But what really concerned us was when Jimmy asked where she had heard that, and Julie said, "I heard it at school, and I believe *them*." This was the first time we had seen a real spirit of doubt try to take hold of our daughter.

We didn't know what to do, so we prayed about it. We asked "God, it is Your will for us to keep Julie in her current school, or should we enroll her in a Christian school?" It wasn't going to be the easiest thing to change schools, and it certainly was going to be more expensive, but God gave us total peace about finding a Christian school and transferring Julie there.

Before you jump to any conclusions, though, we are not saying Christian school is the answer for every family. The school we found for Julie wasn't perfect, not by a long shot, and she was only there for a short time. We learned that you cannot depend on any school, Christian or otherwise, to raise your child. It's nice if the school mirrors your values and beliefs, but it's your job to instill them.

———————

When your child becomes an adult, you should be able to look at them and say, "I have taught you how to watch the gates of your life. I have produced a responsible gatekeeper, and you are going to live the rest of your life safely from the power of the devil and every desire he has over you."

15

Training Maneuvers

In the first two chapters, we shared about the well-known Scripture, "Train up a child in the way he should go, and when he is old he will not depart from it" (Proverbs 22:6). We encourage you to memorize this promise because you will need it when your child is acting the opposite of what they have been taught, refusing to listen to godly counsel, or walking in the sinful ways of the world. Notice the promise does not say a child won't be strong-willed or have a bad attitude. It doesn't say a child won't be tempted to make bad decisions or even succumb to the pleasures of sin. It's during those dark days, months, or even years that parents must hold onto the promise that if they have done their part in training their child in the ways of God, the child will eventually come back to walk in righteousness. It may look hopeless for a time or a season but hold onto the promise.

Every promise of God is conditional upon some act of obedience on your part.

Did you know every promise of God is conditional upon some act of obedience on your part? "If" we do what the Word says, "then" the promise will be fulfilled. We must meet the condition on every promise. In the above Scripture, the condition is training. Children don't need parents just to tell them what to do. They need parents to show them how to do it because "a picture paints a thousand words." In Richard Fugate's book, *What the Bible Says About Child Training*, he makes an interesting observation about the misconceived idea many parents have about raising children:

> Raising a child is not training. Plants and animals are raised. To raise something means to grow it. To raise a child would only consist of feeding, clothing, and protecting him from destruction until he reaches physical maturity. While it is true today that most parents are only raising their children, "raising" does not constitute the training of the soul that God intends.

Ask yourself this question: Are you raising or training your children? We're going to examine three elements of training a child: modeling, communication, and grace. Incorporating these elements into your parenting will allow you to train a child to become the man or woman of God they were created to be.

MODELING

The most powerful issue in training a child is modeling godly behavior. A little girl said to me (Karen) one time, "My mommy and daddy whip us for fighting with each other, but they keep us up all night fighting with each other in their bedroom." These parents were telling their children, "Do as we say, not as we do!" Children quickly recognize that kind of hypocrisy. One way to break a child's spirit is to expect something of them that you are not doing (or not willing to do) yourself.

As a parent, modeling means, "I am going to show you how it's done." What your children see from you is 10 times more powerful than what they hear from you. Telling them things like

"Don't do that," "Don't fight," "Empty the trash," "Go to church," and "Read your Bible" mean nothing unless you show them how to do it.

Tom was working on his car in the driveway, and his five-year-old son, Maddox, was watching every move, wanting to help. When Tom got ready to fill the radiator, he showed Maddox how to slowly turn on the hose. Tom said, "Now, when I tell you, turn on the water; and when I say 'okay,' then turn it off." As directed, Maddox turned on the water slowly. Then Tom proceeded with filling the radiator, and when it was almost full, he called out, "Okay!" But Maddox turned the faucet the wrong way, and the water sprayed all over the engine and all over his father. Angrily, Tom turned to his son and said, "Why didn't you turn it off when I told you to?" Maddox looked at his father with tears in his eyes and said, "But Daddy, you didn't show me how to turn it off!"

How many times do we expect our children to do things the right way when we either haven't shown them how or have only given them partial instructions? How often do we expect more of our children than they are old enough to handle? Children need to be patiently shown how to do things as many times as necessary until they have been trained to do it right.

Your parents' behavior influenced your life in a powerful way, just as your behavior is influencing your children's lives in a powerful way. That is why positive modeling is so important in the training process. When Brent was growing up, every time I (Jimmy) spoke or interacted with Karen in front of him, I knew I was training my son how to treat women. And every time Julie was present, I was teaching her how a woman should be treated by a man. Every time I did anything in front of my children, I was training them what to do. I was modeling it for them.

Do you want your children to grow up to be like you? Actually, it doesn't matter whether you do or don't because they're going to either way. Godly training means, "I am going to show you how to love God. I am going to show you how to respect a woman. I am going to show you how to respect a man. I am going to show you how to submit to authority. I am going to show you how to resolve conflict. I am going to show you about the values of life; and God is the most important, people are the second most important, serving in church is the third most important, and making money is way down on the list. I'm going to model these values for you."

A parent's behavior has a greater determining value on the outcome of that child than any other factor in his life. What are you doing? How do you talk to people? How do you respond when you are angry? What are your attitudes? What are your values?

Your kids are born with a 24-hour video and audio recorder inside of them. They're sitting there recording your life, your values, and your attitudes. You can put them in front of a TV or a computer or send them to school or church, but it is your behavior that has the greatest influence on your children.

A godly parent isn't afraid of replicating themselves in their kids. Once we (Jimmy and Karen) became a united front with the right priorities, we realized that we wanted our children to have a church just like we do, a relationship with the Lord just like we do, a marriage just like we do, etc. Now, Brent and Julie have turned out even better than us, and we are so proud of them. They're better parents than we were. They've taken it to the next level.

A godly parent isn't afraid of replicating themselves in their kids.

Whenever we found an area in our lives that we didn't want Brent and Julie to model, we repented to them, to God, and to each other, and we got that area out of our lives. We were absolutely determined to model godly strengths and values. If you don't want your children to be like you, then examine the areas that need to be changed, repent to your children, to God, and to your spouse. Start modeling the behavior you do want them to follow. It's never too late to start.

COMMUNICATION

Training our child means communicating to them God's love, His Word, and His principles for living from the time they're born to the time they leave your house.

Many studies have been done on how much quality interaction parents have with their children. According to a 2021 report from the United States Bureau of Labor Statistics, "Parents whose youngest child was younger than age 6 spent the most time caring for their children and other household members as a primary activity (2.5 hours per day), while parents whose youngest child was ages 13 to 17 spent the least amount of time doing so (32 minutes)."[1] Now the good news about these numbers is that they have been increasing over the recent decades. Dads, in particular, have spending more time with their children (eight hours per week in 2016 versus 2.5 hours per week in 1965).[2]

But is this quality time? A 2021 study found that "parents only spend 24 minutes more with their children than they do their phones" and "69 percent of parents surveyed feel 'addicted' to their phone."[3] Now, we recognize that cell phones are a part of life for most Americans, and we aren't saying that they or other electronic devices are evil. But you aren't responsible before God for training your phone. You are responsible for training your children, so they must be more important.

As our Brent and Julie were growing up, we (Jimmy and Karen) spent thousands and thousands of hours with them. You may be wondering, *What could you possibly talk about to your children for that long?* We talked about what the Bible says. We talked about what our expectations were. We talked about the questions they had about God and about situations they were facing. If we didn't know the answer, we went and found it, because it was our responsibility to train them in the Word of God.

A crucial part of communication is accountability. Once a standard of behavior has been set and properly communicated to a child, it is important to hold them to that standard. Your child must learn that they are accountable for their words and actions and that every choice has an outcome, whether good or bad. Obviously, a two-year-old does not have the same mental capacity as a 12-year-old, and a parent must set reasonable, age-appropriate expectations. But it's much easier to begin teaching accountability when your child is young and making "little" choices (like cleaning up toys and obeying the first time) than when they are older and making "big" choices (like respecting public property and honoring authority at school). Children who aren't held accountable have no understanding or respect for the weight of their actions, and they grow into reckless teenagers and irresponsible adults.

The purpose of the church and school is to reinforce, not replace, what you're teaching at home.

Don't set your child up for failure. You must hold them accountable, and the way to start is holding yourself accountable. Here's an important point to remember: You can't give something away you don't have. You need to have the wisdom of the Word in you in order to give it to your children. Proverbs 20:7 says, "The righteous *man* walks in his integrity; his children *are* blessed after him." Your children need you to talk to them, to find the answers they need, to encourage them, and to communicate godly expectations. You must be able to say to them, "Here's what God's Word says. I don't expect you to get the information you need from school or from church or from anyone else. I expect you to get it from me." The purpose of the church and school is to reinforce, not replace, what you're teaching at home.

GRACE

If we are going to train our children, we must give them grace as they learn what is right and what is wrong. That means we don't just discipline them for what they've done wrong, but we also reward them for what they've done right.

I (Julie) was always a good student in elementary school, and I made good grades. However, in fourth grade, I had a math teacher that my friends and I just could not stand. She was the worst! So when my dad saw my report card with an F in math, I tried to explain that it wasn't my fault. I wanted him to go to the school and tell the principal just how bad that teacher was. But to my surprise, my dad said, "No, I'm not doing that. I support the teacher." And when I tried to object, he said, "Tough. You will overcome."

As a child I was really frustrated, but now as a parent myself, I understand what my dad was doing. He wasn't allowing me to rebel against authority, and he refused to take up my offense against that math teacher. He taught me, "You will have a good attitude even if your teacher has a bad attitude." And looking back, I realize that if he had gone after every teacher I didn't like, there would have been no survivors!

That's not the end of this story, though. My dad told me, "Julie, if you don't bring this grade up to a C, you're going to be grounded for a month." But then he continued: "But if you make a B, I'll give you $50. If you make an A, I'll give you $100." As a fourth grader, I had never seen that much money, and all I could squeak out was, "You what?" He reiterated, "If you make an A, I'll give you $100. I'll do anything I can to help you learn what you don't know, and if you need a tutor or extra help, we'll get you the help. But I will not allow you to give up. You are going to overcome, and you are going to make good grades."

Well, I took that challenge to heart! In the next six weeks, with the help of a tutor, I pulled my grade up to an A, and I happily claimed my $100. Then my brother realized what was happening, and he wanted in on the deal too! It ended up costing our dad more than he originally bargained for, but it taught us the invaluable lesson that our dad was more than a disciplinarian—he was also a rewarder.

One critical point to understand about the consequence and reward system is that once you make a commitment, you must be consistent in administering it. If you establish a consequence for a wrong action, then follow through on it every time. If you promise a reward, be sure you fulfill your promise. If my dad had not fulfilled his promise to me to pay $100 for my A, I would not have believed him the next time. Broken promises produce broken children. Don't promise what you cannot or will not do.

Maybe you were disciplined harshly or maybe not at all. Maybe you were never rewarded. But God is a loving disciplinarian when we do something wrong, and He is a loving rewarder when we do something right. If it has worked for Him for thousands of years, don't you think it's worth a try in your home? Start today by reprogramming your mind and heart to allow grace to abound in your home with loving discipline and just rewards. Model yourself after your gracious heavenly Father.

———————

Parenting is difficult, but its rewards are great. Pray this prayer with us:

Lord, we thank You for this Word and this promise about training our children. Reveal to us any issue that would cause us not to have the right resources for parenting and heal the pain and hurt caused by these issues. We resolve that we are not going to be bullied by a fallen world, to reject Your Word, or to believe in anything other than Your promises. Lord, Your Word is eternal, and it is powerful. Your Word has a guarantee that it will not return void, and we want to be good models to our children. Even though we're not perfect, we want to be godly. We are committed to train up our children in the way You want them to go. We thank You for the promise, that if we do that, our children will grow up right, and the end result will be a good one. May blessings flow upon our home. In Jesus' name, Amen.

SECTION 3

BATTLEFIELDS

COMMUNICATION DISCIPLINE and SEXUALITY

16

The War for Words

The way we communicate with our children is a critical issue. Our words stretch like a tightrope between life or death for them. Children need an abundant supply of positive and truthful words flowing into their lives in order to develop properly. Satan's desire is to poison, prohibit, or distort the information coming through us to our children, but God's desire is to make our mouths a fountain of life. Our children's future hangs in the balance of who wins the war for our words.

Our children's future hangs in the balance of who wins the war for our words.

Proverbs 18:21 says, "Death and life *are* in the power of the tongue, and those who love it will eat its fruit." Here is a paraphrase of that Scripture: *The power to build up or tear down, to encourage or discourage, to educate or deceive, to nurture or reject, is activated through every word we speak. Words are never neutral. They all embody attitudes, emotions, and values. The person who understands the power of words and commits themselves to positive speech will reap an abundant harvest as a result.*

As a parent, death and life are resident within your tongue. Every word that comes out of your mouth is important, and you will be held accountable for every one of them. Jesus said, "And I tell you this, you must give an account on judgment day for every idle word you speak. The words you say will either acquit you or condemn you" (Matthew 12:36–37 NLT).

Do you know why God holds us in account for every word? It's because every word has meaning. There's no such thing as saying something to your child that "doesn't matter." If you understand the power of words and use them positively, you'll reap positive fruit from them. It works in reverse as well—if you sow negative words, you will reap negative results.

Numerous Scriptures speak of the power of words. Proverbs 16:24 says, "Pleasant words *are like* a honeycomb, sweetness to the soul and health to the bones." And Proverbs 12:18 tells us, "There is one who speaks like the piercings of a sword, but the tongue of the wise *promotes* health." Have you ever been around someone whose mouth was like a sword? You fear being around them because you don't know what they are going to say. Their words are so sharp that your feelings get hurt whenever you are with that person. Proverbs 15:4 says, "Gentle words are a tree of life; a deceitful tongue crushes the spirit" (NLT). You can break your child's spirit through the words you speak to them.

In order to communicate positively with your children, every word you speak to them should fall into one of three categories: praise, kindness, and speaking the truth in love. If it doesn't, you're doing something wrong. These are the biblical standards you should set for yourself and your family.

PRAISE

Psalm 100:4 says we are to "enter into [God's] gates with thanksgiving, *and* into His courts with praise." You will never reach your child's heart without praising them. It's easy to start griping at your kids and talking down to them, but when you find yourself doing that, start looking instead for their blessings. By blessing our children, we create an atmosphere of praise.

We are created in the image of God, and we simply are not going to get into His courts without praising Him. We are God's temple, His dwelling place, and He will not come into a place where there is no praise. Suppose your children haven't picked up their rooms like they were supposed to, and they left a mess in the kitchen again. You start spewing off complaints—"I don't know why nobody around here can do anything right. I have to do it all, and I'm sick of it. From now on everybody in this family can just forget it. I'm not going to be anybody's slave."

We must understand that when we speak negatively, we completely lose our influence with our children. Just as God won't let us into His gates without praise, our children won't either.

Your child reacts the same way when you say things like, "You idiot, why can't you just listen for once? I've told you a million times to clean up your room. You're just a slob. This room looks like a pigsty, and I'm sick of it!" When you speak in an angry, critical tone towards your child and start putting them down, their heart says, "Mom, I'm sorry, but no one's home. Say anything you want. You may make me comply this time, but I've already decided that you're not going to change me because you've hurt my heart."

Your children are created in the image of God, and you should be their number one fan. Don't go digging in the dirt to find all the things they do wrong. Start looking for the gold and praise the things they do right. Say things like "You are so smart. I just knew you could do it!" and "Wow! You are so fast. I've never seen a child so fast." Find what they do right, focus on that, and praise it, praise it, praise it.

A grandmother shared with me (Jimmy) a challenge her daughter was having in disciplining her oldest child. This little granddaughter was very strong-willed, and spanking did not seem to work in changing her stubborn behavior. However, the grandmother discovered that the secret to this girl's heart was in hugging and praising her. If she was told harshly or in a demanding tone to pick up her toys, all the spankings in the world wouldn't budge her. But if her grandmother took her aside and told her what a good girl she was to pick up her toys so well, that little girl would do it willingly and with a smile on her face. She responded to praise and love, but she dug in her heels to harsh or critical words.

Karen and I had special names for our kids growing up. I called Julie "sweet girl." Did she always act sweet? No, I was saying it by faith. I picked a name that described who I wanted her to be and called her by that name. The more I said it, the sweeter Julie got. And today as an adult, she is extremely sweet natured.

I called Brent "sweet boy" until he got older and threatened me never to call him that again! I switched to "big boy" after that, and he lived up to that name as well, standing 6'4" in his bare feet. With these names I was saying to my kids, "I'm going to praise you. I'm going to tell you what's right about you. I'm your number one fan."

When you praise your child, they are drawn to you and want to be around you. We see in Psalm 22:3 that God inhabits the praises of His people. Did you know when someone starts praising God, He shows up? Did you know when you start praising your child, they show up? If the only one who is praising your daughter is some boy in the back seat of a car, she'll find that boy. If the only one praising your son is some antisocial group that abuses drugs and alcohol and listens to bad music, he'll find that group. Your children must know that you are their number one fan, and you think more highly of them than anyone else.

When you praise your child, they are drawn to you and want to be around you.

We will talk about discipline in the coming chapters, but even in the midst of conflict and bad attitudes, keep praising and praising and praising your child. Tell them what they're doing right, and they will start doing more and more things right as time goes along. When we praise, we earn the right to correct. Model the behavior you want your child to follow, train them to have an attitude of praise, and they will follow your lead.

KINDNESS

Kindness is an essential quality in training a child. Proverbs chapter 31 talks about an excellent woman, and verse 26 says, "When she speaks, her words are wise, and she gives instructions with kindness" (NLT). The fruit of the Spirit includes kindness, as you can read in Galatians 5:22. Kindness means you respect the high value and emotions of the person to whom you're speaking.

Imagine one of your kids runs the riding lawn mower right through the flower bed you have spent all spring planting and tending to. You're so angry, and you yell, "You moron! Don't you know any better than to do that? Good grief, I've told you at least a dozen times not to run the mower that fast. Are you so stupid you can't even mow the lawn right just once?" That tirade doesn't exactly communicate kindness, does it? When we start talking down to a person, kindness goes out the window.

If you understand how valuable your child is to God and to you and how precious their emotions are, then you're going to get your emotions under control first. You're going to carefully choose the right words before you speak, and you're also going to monitor your tone, gestures, and facial expressions. Yelling is not kind. Crude gestures are not kind. And hateful facial expressions, like sneering or scowling, are not kind.

When you're unkind to your child, you're teaching them that they are not valuable, and then they'll begin to think and act like they're not valuable. So many children today haven't been shown kindness, so they lash out at others with meanness and insensitivity. They are cynical and untrusting of others. Far too many see no value in life at all, and in 2020, the second leading cause of death in young people ages 10–14 was suicide.[1]

None of us are perfect parents, and most (if not all) of us have said things in anger to our children that have wounded them. Children need to see and hear their parents admit when they mess up: "I'm so sorry for saying that. I never want to hurt you. Will you please forgive me?" Having an open relationship in which your children can tell you that you have hurt their feelings is an important aspect of the maturing process. It teaches them how to handle conflict and emotions in a healthy manner without fear.

Through the words we speak to our children, our hearts and minds connect together. It is a moment-by-moment choice to speak words of encouragement, blessing, healing, affection, and kindness. When you make that choice, you are speaking life into your family.

SPEAKING THE TRUTH IN LOVE

Let not mercy and truth forsake you;
Bind them around your neck,
Write them on the tablet of your heart,
And so find favor and high esteem
In the sight of God and man (Proverbs 3:3–4).

But, speaking the truth in love, may grow up in all things into Him who is the head—Christ (Ephesians 4:15).

Every successful relationship must be balanced with truth and love. Truth is the essential ingredient that bears a standard and prevents violation or moral degradation. Love is the essential ingredient that values and elevates the heart connection. Truth and love are inseparable partners. By itself, truth is cruel, intimidating, and counterproductive. It is a harsh taskmaster with no loyal subjects.

Love by itself is a cheerleader without a team—a spineless organism without strength of definition. But together, love is the ointment that makes the presence of truth bearable.

Every successful relationship must be balanced with truth and love.

Consider these profound statements:

- Relationships of truth without love dry up.
- Relationships of love without truth blow up.
- Relationships of truth and love grow up.

When I (Jimmy) first started pastoring a growing congregation of 900-plus people, I was very insecure. I did my best, but I'm as human as anyone else, and I can remember two specific times that someone pushed me to the edge and made me mad. I became unkind and said things I shouldn't have said. In both cases I had to go back later and repent for my words.

I have never seen truth without love produce anything positive. As a pastor dealing with all those people, I learned to handle a difficult person by saying, "I love you, but in this church, we're going to do things this way. Now, if you want to go somewhere else, that's fine. I want you to know I love you either way." When I confronted a staff member or someone who had done something wrong, the first thing I did was affirm that person: "I love you. I really care for you. I want you to know that you're valuable here." If Karen and I are having a disagreement or talking something out, the first thing I do is say, "I love you, and I want you to know I appreciate you. We're on the same team, but that hurt my feelings."

When you're applying truth to your children, you need to constantly keep it in an atmosphere of love. You don't respect someone who doesn't tell you the truth, do you? You don't like people who are honest in a crude way either, do you? Here's what you do like: people who will tell you how they feel in a very careful, loving manner. Your children feel the same way. Speak the truth in love.

Use the power of your words to reap a godly harvest for your children. Decide to praise them and be kind to them. Treat them with tremendous value when speaking to them. If you have to say something tough and apply truth in a corrective fashion, make sure it's coated with how much you love your children and how valuable they are to you.

Some of you are still hurting over a word that was spoken to you years ago. Some of you are battling feelings of self-hate or low self-esteem because of things your parents said to you that stripped you of your dignity and made you feel worthless. I (Karen) cannot describe to you how much shame I carried throughout my childhood into my adult life because of the words spoken over me by my parents. It didn't matter how often Jimmy told me that he loved me or that I was beautiful. All I could see in the mirror was a worthless, unlovable woman. That's how powerful words are. It took years and years of healing to be able to love myself.

I (Jimmy) struggled to help Karen because it was hard to believe her parents could say those kinds of things about such a good person like her. In fact, if anyone had been deserving of being put down, it was me! I was worthy of all kinds of bad press, but I never heard my parents say anything bad about me. Sometimes when I'd done something bad, I'd hide around the corner listening to my parents talk, expecting to hear them say, "Well, Jimmy is just a total idiot. You know, he did this and this and this." But every time my parents talked about me, it was in a positive manner, even when I didn't deserve it. In retrospect, I never had a problem of low self-esteem. I look back, and I deeply respect my parents. They never put me down or criticized me, and that made it easier for me to follow their pattern with my own children while keeping a proper balance of love and truth.

Jesus is full of grace and truth. As a result, we are drawn to Him, and His influence on our lives is redemptive and powerful. A home full of grace and truth will also be a place to which family members are drawn. A balanced family will be redemptive and powerful, filled with lasting joy and loving progress. And, like God Himself, a family full of grace and truth is invincible and eternal.

17

Communication Challenges

What would you say is the number one cause of divorce and dysfunctional family relationships? Some of you will say financial problems, and others may say adultery, but after more than 40 years as a pastor and teacher, I (Jimmy) can truthfully say that poor communication is the number one root cause. Strife over finances, the trap of adultery, and all the other problems related to broken relationships are the result of poor communication. Most families don't know how to communicate in a positive, effective manner. When adults don't know how to talk to each other, how can they expect children to do any better?

Family Patterns

Children learn how to talk from their parents and other family members.

Children learn how to talk from their parents and other family members. In the previous chapter we discussed communicating praise, kindness, and truth and love to our children. Does that describe the way your parents communicated to you? If it does, then your parents were good communicators and worthy of emulation. If it doesn't, then your parents didn't model positive communication for you.

We had a friend who was one of the most negative people I've ever met. She was a precious lady, but she saw everything from a negative perspective. Interestingly enough, she criticized her mother for being "the most negative person in the world." We thought, *Well, there may be a runner-up!* This woman had been trained by her mother's constant negativity.

If you realize that your parents' communication patterns were wrong, then do what we talked about in the earlier chapters of this book—forgive your parents, break off those iniquities and inner vows, and put your eyes on Jesus. Pray, "Lord, teach me how to communicate according to Your Word."

Personalities

Jimmy and I (Karen) have opposite personalities. I am very laid back, and for much of my life, if I was hurt or offended, I would just stew on it instead of saying anything about it. It's like I would put my feelings in a pressure cooker and let them simmer for a long time until the pressure finally blew the lid off. I had a really long fuse, but when it finally blew, all the emotional hurt and baggage I had packed away came tumbling out. As a young wife and mother, I had to learn to be more honest and forthright with sharing my feelings.

On the other hand, I (Jimmy) am an open book, and if there's an issue or situation that I don't like, I feel very comfortable addressing it. In the first few years of being married to Karen, I had to learn *not* to say everything I was thinking. Here is the Scripture the Lord convicted me with regarding how I treated my wife: "Husbands, love your wives, just as Christ also loved the church and gave Himself for her, that he might sanctify and cleanse her with the washing of water by the word" (Ephesians 5:25–26). My understanding of that verse was, *I'll hose Karen down with my words. I'll get her washed off really good!* But the Lord spoke to me and said, "No, Jimmy, I'm washing My bride ceremonially. I'm taking the Word, and I'm gently washing her." The Lord told me I was too harsh with my mouth because I was trying to produce immediate results. He said, "Jimmy, it's going to take a lifetime of my Word in your life to clean you up, and I'm being gentle with you. Now you be gentle with Karen." I needed to learn to be slower to speak and gentler when I did speak.

The two of us learned how to communicate with each other in an open, honest, and loving manner. God made each of us unique, and He created the differences in us to complement and balance each other. Where I am strong, Karen is weak, and vice versa. Where I'm slow to listen, Karen is a great listener. Where I'm quick to make a decision, Karen needs more time to think about it, and sometimes her caution saves us from making a mistake. I balance Karen, and she balances me.

It's the same with our children. We must learn to adapt our different personality styles and communicate in ways that allow each child to blossom. When I (Julie) hit the teenage years, I definitely pushed my mom's buttons into the red zone at times. That's when my dad stepped in. He helped my mom to see if she was being unreasonable, and he disciplined me if I was being uncooperative and disobedient. And my mom helped my dad with Brent in the same way.

If you weaponize the words of your mouth and emotionally beat your children into the ground, the message you are sending is that parents are harsh and cruel. Your child will picture God as a dictator who doesn't care about anyone else's feelings. If you're sweet for four or five days and then just unload on your children, you teach them that God is unpredictable or even schizophrenic. Children who live in that kind of an atmosphere think, *God likes me sometimes, but sometimes He hates me. God is so moody!*

The truth is that God's mercies are new every morning (see Lamentations 3:22–23). If something is bothering you in your relationship with your child, get it out into the open, but always do it in a loving way. Resolve it and forgive so you're able to move on in love.

Discipline

It is critical to resolve discipline issues in a timely manner so that they won't harden your heart toward your child. Ephesians 4:26 says, "Be angry, and do not sin: do not let the sun go down on your wrath." You must take care of disciplinary issues the day they happen and forgive your child before you go to bed.

Have you ever gone to bed mad at your kids? Some people might say, "Well, that's just life. I'm constantly mad at my kids." Well, that mindset is extremely dangerous. When you go to bed angry, the anger compacts down in your spirit. When you wake up the next morning, it has become more a part of your subconscious, which is where unkindness and anger linger. Angry people are people with unresolved issues in their lives. No matter what form of discipline you choose, you need to apply it and forgive the child right then.

> **No matter what form of discipline you choose, you need to apply it and forgive the child right then.**

No one will ever offend you as many times as your child does. Unforgiveness is like poison manifesting in angry, explosive, cynical, sarcastic, or critical words. You must constantly forgive your child and deal with discipline issues *today*.

Correction and discipline must be relational. Our words can beat our children down and strip them of their self-worth. Be careful when you are tired or stressed out and come upon your child doing something wrong. Have you ever heard Zig Ziglar tell his famous "kick the cat" story? It illustrates how stress and frustration get passed on from person to person. The president of a company felt some changes were needed, so he called a meeting and set higher standards for punctuality and attendance. Then he told the employees that he would hold himself to this standard as an example. Later in the week at a lunch meeting, time got away from this president. In his rush to get back to the office on time, he got a speeding ticket, and boy, was he mad. He came into the office and chewed out his sales manager. The sales manager was very upset, so he went out and gave his secretary a tongue lashing and issued some very unreasonable orders. The secretary was furious, so she dumped her anger and workload onto the switchboard operator. The operator did the extra work but went home in a bad mood. When she walked in the door, she saw her son watching television and noticed a big tear in his brand-new jeans. She never even gave him a chance to explain before she read him the riot act and levied an extreme punishment of no dinner that night and no more television privileges for three weeks. The boy was so upset that he ran up the stairs in a huff. The family cat was walking down the hallway just then, and the boy kicked it in the tail and said, "You get out of here! You've probably been up to some no good yourself!"

Have you ever come home from a bad day at work and chewed your child out without waiting for any explanations and then doled out an unreasonable punishment? We must remember this formula: rules – relationship = rebellion. When we're disciplining our children, we need to do it in a relational way, or rebellion will be the result. The less relational your discipline is, the more severe it is going to be, because you're going to try to produce results as quickly as you can without spending the time with that child. If you don't take time to talk it out, you're making a big mistake.

Discipline takes patience. If you try to produce immediate results in your child, you'll break that child's spirit, because children have foolishness in their hearts (see Proverbs 22:15). It takes years of consistent discipline to drive that foolishness out. If you say, "No, I'm going to drive it out right now," you'll end up damaging that child, maybe even for life.

Discipline also takes faith. because you are going to have to believe that investing in your child and doing what is right will eventually pay off. When you say to your child, "I'm going to discipline you, and after the discipline is over, I expect you to do what I say," it doesn't mean that their attitude is exactly where you want it to be. It doesn't mean that they are mature, or wise, or doing everything you expect. It just means you're going to keep holding the standard and enforcing it, all while understanding it's going to take an entire process for it to work. Julie and Brent were both in college before we finally saw what we had done for 18 to 20 years kick in. We never saw it when they were children. Were they good kids? Yes, but they also were normal kids.

We had all the typical teenage struggles with Julie growing up, but she was a good girl, and we were proud of her. When she left for college, I remember we were praying for her, and we had a certain mental image of her growing up. Her personality changed in college, and she truly turned into a woman of God. Talking to her on the phone and being around her when she was at home, we realized that what we had prayed for and tried to produce in her for years was finally starting to happen. That's when you sit back and go, *There is a God! His way really does work!*

You're going to have to hold to your standard every day, year in and year out, with a lot of love, a lot of discipline, a lot of time, a lot of effort, and a lot of training. Finally, one day, you will produce a woman or a man of God, and you will know it was all worth it. When we (Jimmy and Karen) watched Julie and then Brent graduate, we looked at them and thought, *No one can take out of them what's been invested in them, and we know it's going to pay off.* And in both of their lives, it's paid off! It will pay off in your child's life too.

18

The Discipline Battle

Parenting has always been a challenge, but there are more complex parenting issues today than any previous generations have faced. The dramatic changes and divergence from the traditional family unit has increased the number of divorced families, single parent families, blended families, and even same-sex parents having families via adoption and in vitro fertilization. Technological advances in genetics once thought to be impossible are bringing ethical issues relating to multiple births, proxy birth mothers, and even cloning to the forefront.

Parents and children have never faced more temptations, social obstacles, deception, and fear than they do today. Children are becoming sexually active at younger and younger ages, and they face the reality of STDs and revenge porn. In 2022 alone, there were 300 school shooting incidents in the United States.[1] And we've already mentioned how suicide is one of the leading causes of death in young people.

How can parents protect their children and prepare them for such a rapidly changing and uncertain world? The only answer is seeking the power and perspective for parenting from God's Word. By building our families upon the promises found in Scripture, we lay a sure foundation for success. As we are seeing so many children out of control and families in crisis, a major contributing factor is the lack of loving discipline in the home.

This may sound strange, but loving discipline—and yes, that includes spanking done the right way—tells a child that they are loved. You may be familiar with Proverbs 13:24, which says, "Those who spare the rod of discipline hate their children. Those who love their children care enough to discipline them" (NLT). But you also need to know Proverbs 29:15, which says, "The rod and rebuke give wisdom, but a child left to *himself* brings shame to his mother." If we correct our children, we give them wisdom. That's a promise. But if we leave them to their own choices and don't discipline them, they will bring shame to our families.

> # Loving discipline—and yes, that includes spanking done the right way—tells a child that they are loved.

Proverbs 29:17 says, "Correct your son, and he will give you rest; Yes, he will give delight to your soul." A disciplined child will give their parents peace and rest and will be a delight to them. The opposite of rest is anxiety and stress. If you do not correct your child, they will ruin your life and theirs, not just as a child but also as an adult. All the comfort you think you are producing by not taking action now will be robbed from you by what they do later on.

There are four important issues that need to be considered by every parent in addressing the matter of child discipline:

No Excuse for Abuse

While we believe in spanking as a form of discipline, we absolutely do not condone child abuse. Abuse subjects children to harmful physical, emotional, or spiritual influences that demonstrate something to them that is unlike God's nature. Proper spanking, however, protects children and reveals two truths: there are real and painful consequences they will meet later in life if they live irresponsibly, and God punishes those who disobey Him and His Word. Therefore, spanking is helpful to a child when it is done in a proper manner.

Proper spanking is illustrated in a scenario like this: you have warned your son, Johnny, who is old enough to understand your expectations, concerning something. You have told him that if he disobeys you in this matter, he will be spanked. Then he disobeys. You take Johnny to a private area. Never yell or scream unless it is in an emergency, such as a warning of some kind. ("Watch out! A car is coming!") Also, never discipline your child in public. Rather, when he disobeys you, calmly lead him to his bedroom or a private place.

When you get there, say something like, "Johnny, I told you not to ride your bike in the street, and I saw you out there just a minute ago. You disobeyed me. I want you to bend over the bed. I am going to have to spank you."

By this time, Johnny may be crying, begging, bargaining, or twisting around. As the parent, you keep a straight face and control your emotions. With a paddle, wooden spoon, or wooden rod (not your hand or a random instrument), you swat the child on the bottom hard enough to cause discomfort but not hard enough to cause damage.

Once you have finished the spanking, you put Johnny on your lap or sit him down beside you and hug him. You tell him you love him and forgive him, and you do not want him to disobey you anymore. Then you pray for him. When you have finished, you say, "Johnny, I love you. You are a very good boy. Now, go and have fun!"

Without love and proper training, parents who abusively spank their children typically have waited until their emotions are out of control. Abusive parents warn a child over and over with something like, "Billy, you do that one more time, and you're going to get a whipping!"

Because the parent doesn't follow through, Billy learns not to respect what is said, and sadly, the parents wait until Billy pushes them to the edge of their control before doing something. Then they do too much.

Listen, parents: when God tells you He is going to do something, He always does it. Therefore, when you don't follow through with what you tell your children, you are demonstrating unfaithfulness and dishonesty. This will cause major problems in being able to get your child to respect and obey you, and as your child gets older, they will have a distorted image of God.

Biblical discipline is *never* abusive. It never means flailing a child. It never means holding them down and beating them, causing marks or bruises on their body or things like that. It never means yelling at a child, calling them names, or disciplining them in public.

Biblical discipline is *never* abusive.

Do not lie to a child to instill fear into them. For example, when a child misbehaves or disobeys, do not say that God is going to kill them or "get them" or that their body parts will fall off. Lovingly speak truth to children and follow through with what you say. This way you can stay in control as you responsibly discipline your children.

The Anti-Spanking Lobby

There has been an onslaught of teaching in the past several decades instructing parents not to spank their children. These so-called experts in child-rearing methods teach that spanking causes children to resent and hate their parents and provokes them to adopt violent lifestyles. By not spanking children, their "natural" goodness will be expressed.

In addition to being in total disagreement with God's Word, there are many problems with the philosophy of these secular, and even sometimes Christian, "gurus" of child behavior.

First, these humanistic "philosophies" constantly change, so they cannot be presenting absolute truth. For example, years ago, parenting "experts" discouraged mothers from nursing their babies. They declared that formula was healthier. Then, it all changed, and mothers were encouraged to nurse their babies because breastmilk was healthier. Parenting philosophies may change, but absolute truth is constant.

Second, experts who tell parents not to spank their children directly contradict the Word of God. The Bible has much to contribute to the issue of parenting and child discipline. Read Proverbs 13:24; 22:6; 23:13; 29:15; Ephesians 6:1–4; and Hebrews 12:11.

The basis of almost all anti-spanking teaching today is humanism. This political and religious philosophy teaches that we do not have a sin nature. Rather, everyone, including you and your child, has inherent goodness inside them. According to this philosophy, if you can just put your child in the correct environment, his "natural goodness" will come out.

While we agree that children should be in a positive environment, the truth is that we all have sinful natures that must be corrected and held in check. Without the proper discipline and restraints, our children will self-destruct if left to themselves.

If children are inherently good, then why are they naturally selfish and rebellious? From the day my (Julie's) children were born, Cory and I loved and cared for them. However, they weren't "naturally" kind with their friends. We had to teach them. It was not "natural" for our girls to obey us—we had to teach them. It was not "natural" for them to have good attitudes—we had to teach them. People are not naturally good; they are naturally sinful.

Isaiah 53:6 says, "We all, like sheep, have gone astray, each of us has turned to our own way; and the Lord has laid on him [Jesus] the iniquity of us all" (NIV). Not only are all people naturally prone to sin, but the only way goodness comes into our lives is when we follow Jesus. According to Galatians 5:22, goodness is a fruit of the Holy Spirit's presence in our lives. Without Him, we may be good compared to someone worse than us, but we are not truly good and certainly not good enough to be saved by our goodness.

A third fallacy anti-spanking teachers have is their reasoning that spanking causes a child to become violent. While we do agree that abuse will affect a child adversely, we do not agree that spanking makes children violent. Correct discipline teaches a child to respect others and to restrain their own behavior. An excellent argument against the spanking-causes-violence school of thought is this: if you get a ticket for speeding and have to pay a $100 fine, are the police teaching you to be reckless with your money? After you pay the fine, will you get an irresistible urge to start giving money away? Of course not! You are fined for speeding to get your attention and restrain your behavior. This is the same reason why parents spank children.

Spanking Is Not Always the Answer

Parents must be careful not to use one method (like spanking) as a cure-all for every problem. For example, sometimes a child's behavior is communicating an unmet need or hurt. A parent needs to be sensitive to children to know when something wrong is going on inside of them.

There are times when another form of discipline may be more effective than spanking. We aren't huge fans of grounding, because this method punishes the parent along with the child. But we do believe grounding is appropriate at times, as well as the withdrawal of certain privileges, added responsibilities, and other creative ways of teaching our children to behave.

We always need to be careful that discipline does not damage the children or subject them to an ungodly influence. On the other hand, we must make sure our forms of discipline get their attention and make them think twice next time.

Parents Must Be in Agreement

When parents do not agree on how they discipline, or when one parent does not support the other, there is an extremely harmful influence on children and on the marriage. Rather than leaving the discipline to one parent, most parents should think about, pray about, and involve themselves in the discipline of the children.

Both parents' feelings and beliefs should be heard and respected, for they both bring an important and legitimate perspective to the discussion of discipline. Once both parents have expressed their feelings, an agreement must be reached and followed through consistently in disciplining the children. Neither parent should be the sole disciplinarian. When one parent disciplines a child, the other parent should back them up. If there is any concern or disagreement, it should be expressed privately.

It is unhealthy for a child to grow up in a home where the parents are in constant disagreement over the matter of discipline. It is also unhealthy when one parent becomes the "fun" one and the other one becomes the disciplinarian. You can't have a "good cop" and a "bad cop." Even if it means compromise, parents must find a point of agreement and support each other.

Neither parent should be the sole disciplinarian.

Never allow a significant difference to develop in how you and your spouse express love or enforce discipline. Your children need both of you to be affectionate with them, and they need both of you to discipline them. Sometimes when the kids reach a certain age, the father has to be the one who enforces the discipline, simply based on size. But you are both empowered to discipline. You both support each other's discipline.

19

The Purpose of Discipline

The purpose of biblical child discipline is fourfold:

1. to protect children from their sin nature
2. to instill character and moral values
3. to prepare them for reality and success
4. to help them understand and accept God

Protect Children from Their Sin Nature

We must protect our children because they are not able to do it themselves.

We must protect our children because they are not able to do it themselves. Children are precious, but in the blink of an eye, they'll stick a bobby pin in a light socket, drink bleach (aka poison), put their hand on a hot stove, or run out in the street in front of a car. Children don't understand how dangerous things are and what the consequences are for their behavior. They will do things that they just shouldn't do.

Discipline can save a child's life and protect them from pain, trauma, disappointment, and even failure. Yes, every child has the potential for greatness, but in order for that potential to be realized successfully, parents must restrain the child's foolish and sinful nature.

I (Jimmy) remember the first time I ever corrected Julie. I don't recall exactly how old she was, but she was walking, and she had quite a little attitude. We were at my grandmother's house, and Julie was walking beside the window ledge where my grandmother had a collection of little china cups and saucers. Now, Karen and I never rearranged our house around our children. We did lock cabinets and use safety measures, but we never put away our valuable things because we taught our children to respect things in our home and in other people's homes.

Julie was looking at one particular china cup, and then she glanced over at me. I said, "Don't touch that, honey." She looked back at that cup and then back at me. I could tell she wanted it badly. I said, "Don't touch it, honey, or Daddy will spank your hand." Now, I had never spanked her before. She looked at that cup again and back at me, and then she reached toward the cup and grabbed it. I walked over, took her little hand, and lightly swatted it. You would have thought it was the end of the world! As she cried, I repeated, "Don't touch that cup, honey." I didn't move the cup. I just stood right there with Julie until she understood that touching the cup would always have a negative consequence.

Doing little things like that as a child is growing up lets them know, "When Mom or Dad say something, I better respond to their voice." Later on, it might not be touching a china cup. It might be poking at an electrical outlet or reaching for a hot cup of coffee. The child might be pedaling out of the driveway on their bicycle when you see a car coming and you yell, "Stop!" We must train our children, "Listen to my voice and do what I say immediately." It literally will protect them from their own sin nature and their own foolishness. It may even be the difference between life and death.

Instill Character and Moral Values

It is important to train children to respect other people and authority in general. In our (Jimmy and Karen's) generation, a spanking at school meant a worse one when we got home. Today, though, teachers have little to no authority to discipline. If something happens at school, parents take it out on the teachers. We taught Julie and Brent, "You're going to respect authority. If the teacher does something immoral or illegal, come tell us. In the meantime, you submit." We trained them to have moral character and to respond appropriately to authority.

Truthfulness is the number one rule in my (Julie's) house. Lying is the ultimate "no-no," and there is no such thing as a "little white lie." When our girls were still living at home, Cory and I let them have almost anything they wanted to eat in the pantry. The only exception was this little basket of treats. Now, we never made a big deal about food and weight; rather, our family talked about how food either makes you feel good or makes you feel poorly. As parents, we didn't want our girls to feel poorly, so we limited the number of treats they were allowed to eat every day.

One of our girls would frequently sneak into the pantry, usually at night, and take a treat. We might not realize it until later, but then when we confronted her, she would lie about it. This went on for years, and I started to think that maybe I was being too strict. *After all, it's just a treat,* I tried to convince myself. But the treat wasn't the issue, and we all knew it. The issue was the disobedience and the lying. Our daughter was being stubborn, and letting her get away with it would not help her in the long run. So Cory and I kept correcting her, even as we wondered, *Is she ever going to get it?*

I am happy to report that our daughter did eventually "get it"! And both she and her sister have a healthy relationship with food and with Cory and me today. Again, our parenting was never about focusing on the outside. It was about focusing on the inside and teaching our girls that lying is a dangerous habit. The father of lies is Satan himself, and he loves to lure God's children into trouble by lying.

Parents, lying is an area in which you must guard yourself constantly to model godly behavior. Too many times parents punish a child for lying, but then when the phone rings, they say to their child, "If it's for me, tell them I'm not home!" Be careful of the mixed messages you send to your children.

Be careful of the mixed messages you send to your children.

Work ethic was another important character trait in our family. From the time Brent and I were little, our parents had us do chores: cleaning our rooms, taking out the trash, washing dishes, etc. When I turned 16 years old, I started working for my grandparents in their appliance business so I could purchase my first car. Our family also worked together on projects around the house. My parents were not slave drivers, but they trained us to have a good work ethic. We were always expected to be on time, give our very best effort no matter the task, and keep a cheerful attitude.

Sadly, not enough emphasis is placed on cultivating a good work ethic in today's world. I (Jimmy) once came across these insightful statements about work:

1. **"Education covers a lot of ground, but it won't cultivate any of it."**

   A farmer who had a family of boys made them work right alongside him. A neighbor commented one day that it wasn't necessary to work the boys so hard. The farmer said to the neighbor, "I'm not growing crops, I'm growing boys." Too many parents in America are growing couch potatoes instead of productive contributors to society and, more importantly, to the kingdom of God. Knowing how to work and being motivated to do their best at whatever they are doing builds confidence and a positive self-image in children.

2. **"The Successful Family has Work as the father and Integrity as the mother. If you can get along with the 'parents,' you won't have any trouble with the rest of the family."**

Consideration of other people and their feelings is another important character trait that must be instilled in children. When they don't respect others, they must be disciplined. Children are not naturally considerate; in fact, they can be downright mean. They must be trained to share and consider others before themselves.

Prepare Them for Reality and Success

Is the world going to conform itself around your children? Absolutely not. Your child is going to have to learn to respect authority in the workplace. They're going to have to learn that the police don't care who they are, they're not a favored citizen, and if they're doing something wrong, they're going to be punished.

When our family went to a store, we had a specific ritual each time. As I (Jimmy) drove up and parked, Julie and Brent would be in the back seat, not always with the best attitude toward one another. Karen and I would look at them and say, "We're going to go into this store, and we want you to stay next to us. If you're going to do anything, we want you to ask us first; and if you touch anything in there, we'll spank you." We would walk into the store, and our children would stand next to us because they knew if they didn't, they would be disciplined when they got outside to the car.

It hurts our hearts to hear people say, "What a horrible child! I feel sorry for those parents." What they should be saying is, "I feel sorry for that child for having horrible parents who allow them to act that way." I (Jimmy) used to sell appliances, and some of our customers' children terrorized the store. The most pathetic thing I witnessed was people saying, "Billy, put the microwave down, please. Billy, please get out of the refrigerator. Billy, please get your sister out of that dryer. Honey, please don't do that." Now, I said please to my children when I was asking them for something, such as "Honey, would you please bring me a glass of water?" When I was telling them to do something, I lost the please and said, "Don't touch that refrigerator." They would turn around and make eye contact with me, and when they did, I would say, "Come here." They knew when I said, "Come here," I meant, "Come here." Children of any age can understand simple voice commands.

Karen and I trained our children this way: "When you go out in public, you will respect other people's property. When you go out in the real world, you must learn to restrain your desires. We are teaching you how to succeed." One of the reasons we disciplined Brent and Julie was to make them pro-social and not antisocial, so they would understand that the world is not going to conform around them. If you don't discipline your children, the world will do it for you, and the world's discipline is severe. Your discipline is going to be much more gracious than the world's will be because yours will be mixed with love.

Help Them Understand and Accept God

Parents are the first image of God children ever see. Is God a disciplinarian? Absolutely! Hebrews 12:5–6 says, "My son, do not make light of the Lord's discipline, and do not lose heart when he rebukes you, because the Lord disciplines the one he loves, and he chastens everyone he accepts as his son" (NIV). Because God loves us, He disciplines us. When the Lord says, "If you do this, this is going to be the consequence," you can be sure He means it. When God says something, He will follow through on what He says because

He does not lie. The Lord is merciful, but He is also faithful to His standards, and He can discipline in very effective ways.

Our children must be taught there is absolute right and wrong. The majority of "Christians" in America today do not believe in absolute truth, and humanistic ideology has crept into the churches and eroded the moral fiber of our families. The Bible teaches absolute truth, and we must base our discipline and training on such truth. This is what you must teach your children:

> Lying is wrong. Murder is wrong. Immorality is wrong. Why? Because God says they're wrong, and He's a holy God. I am disciplining you to help you understand the nature of God. I love you, and God loves you, and I'm going to discipline you because God is also a disciplinarian. When God says don't do something, He means it.

> I'm your parent. You're going to call God Father later in life, but right now I'm your parent. I love you, and I'm going to train you. I'm going to be a good role model for you. When you disobey me, you're going to suffer the consequences because when you disobey God, you'll suffer even greater consequences.

A parent's behavior has more power and influence on a child's concept of God than anything else.

A parent's behavior has more power and influence on a child's concept of God than anything else. If your parents were mean, it's easy for you to believe God is that way. If your parents were very detached and didn't show love, it's hard for you to believe that God is caring. Here is what a godly parent should want their children to see: an authority figure who is extremely loving and kind and involved in their lives *and* someone who means what they say. Your children need to know that if they violate your standards, they will suffer the consequences every single time. You are trying to introduce them to God, and that's the way He is. He loves them with an unconditional love. He cares about them and wants to be actively involved in every aspect of their lives. When He says something, He means what He says, and He'll follow through.

———————

Parenting is a big responsibility. What we do shapes the lives of our children for their todays on earth and for their tomorrows in eternity. God knew how difficult a job it would be for us, and that is why He left us His Word and His Holy Spirit to help us. Godly discipline may be the difference between life and death for our children now and for eternity.

20

Discipline Strategies, Part 1

Almost 100 percent of the discipline questions we receive from parents are "how to" questions. This chapter is about four simple discipline principles that work in all cases and are easy to remember. We call them the four Cs of discipline.

CLARITY

Always communicate clearly and in a relational manner when disciplining your children. The way you do this will vary depending on their age. Little ones from birth to three or four years old must be trained to respond to your voice commands. Since their understanding is limited, you can't explain things to them, and often, there simply isn't time.

If a child is reaching up to touch a hot burner on the stove, are you going to say, "Don't touch that burner because there's 220 volts of alternating current pulsating through a 12-inch diameter on top of the stove, and it has potential to cause major burns on your little hands?" Of course not. You're going to say, "No, don't touch that." Later on, you can explain what "hot" means, but when children are very young, an explanation isn't always necessary or appropriate. They don't understand why they can't drink what's in the little bottle under the sink that has a skull and crossbones on it. Telling them, "That's poison" doesn't mean anything to their little minds, but they can grasp, "No, don't touch, or you will get a spanking."

Years ago, I (Jimmy) heard a preacher friend share this funny story that illustrates the understanding level of toddlers. While visiting a family who had a small toddler, the preacher happened to walk into the kitchen just in time to see the mother throw a small pill on the floor. The toddler who was sitting nearby quickly reached out, grabbed the pill, and stuffed it in his mouth with a big grin. Rather shocked at what he saw, the preacher said, "Why did you do that?" The mother responded, "Well, when I try to make him take the pill, he fights me, and won't open his mouth. But if I throw it on the floor, he scarfs it up as soon as it hits the floor." I'm sure every parent can relate to that. Some may wish they had thought of trying it!

As children get older and their understanding level matures, we do need to explain the rules and the consequences in language they can clearly understand. Don't ever discipline your children for something they don't understand. Explain the rules and consequences to them clearly. "I want you to make your bed. You have 15 minutes, and if you don't make your bed by then, there will be a consequence of [insert whatever consequence is appropriate]." Then ask them to repeat it back to you to verify they are listening and understand. This thoroughly negates one of the tactic for which kids are most famous—"I didn't hear what you said."

Don't ever discipline your children for something they don't understand.

Those issues of honoring each other are so important. For years Jimmy and I played intermediary between Brent and Julie. I really do wish that when they were young, we had made a rule that said, "You honor each other, and if you don't, this is the consequence." Our home would have been more peaceful, and Julie and Brent would have learned how to adjust to each other's differences with much less conflict.

CONSISTENCY

We cannot say enough about the importance of consistency in discipline. Every single time a child violates the rule, they must be disciplined. Inconsistency is the number one cause of a child not obeying their parents. You say, "Maddie, don't do that. Maddie, I'm not going to warn you anymore. Maddie, I'm only going to say it one more time. Maddie, I said don't do that. Maddie! I'm going to punish you in just one minute!" If you've done that, or you've ever heard it done, you know how fruitless that kind of one-sided conversation is.

Kids learn the system very quickly. They know the volume has to increase about three or four more decibels before anything happens. *I think I've got about four more warnings. I'm gambling on the fact I've got about four more warnings.* Then one day you're in a worse mood than you were when you were warning 15 times, and you only give your child three warnings before you lose it on them. Your child is confused and can't figure out what happened to make Mom or Dad go crazy.

A young woman came into my (Jimmy's) office one day in tears. Her husband had left her with three adorable little kids. She said, "I hate to admit this, but I hate my children. I literally hate them." I handed her a tissue, and she said, "They terrorize me. They're little monsters." She just sat there sobbing, and then she continued: "They don't do anything I say. My husband is gone. They know how to push every button on me that just makes me a blithering idiot. I'm the only one there, and sometimes I hate them. I'm afraid I'm going to abuse them or something."

We talked for a little while about discipline, and she admitted she didn't know how to do it. She said, "They wreck the house and won't pick up after themselves." I said, "Well, let me tell you what to do. Let's just try something new, and I'll train you how to discipline these kids. Is it a normal problem every night that they won't pick up their toys?" She said, "Oh, they just destroy the room, and they won't do anything I say." I said, "Here's what you do: walk in tonight and in a very calm voice say, 'Kids, you have 10 minutes to pick up your toys, and if you don't, Mommy's going to spank you.'" I explained to her, "You're going to do two things. First, you're going to teach them how to tell time. They're going to learn how long 10 minutes is. Second, you're going to teach them to obey your voice. Now, walk out of the room for 10 minutes. When 10 minutes is up, walk back in and say, 'Come here, honey.' One by one take them into another room and spank them. Bring them back in and say, 'Now you have five minutes to pick up your toys. Get them picked up.' In five minutes, about the time you are through with the third one, the first one's time is up. Go back in and if they haven't picked up their toys, you take them out of the room one at a time, spank them again, and then come back and say, 'Do it now.' Keep going through the same process all over again until they obey your voice."

She said, "I can do that?" I said, "You'd better believe you can do that. You go home tonight and all week long every time you tell a child something to do, say it in a calm tone of voice, tell them what the consequence is, and follow through every single time." This lady left my office. When she came back a week later, the first words out of her mouth were, "My children are angels."

Let me tell you another story; this one about my cousin. Our grandmother was baking chocolate chip cookies, and she told us not to eat those cookies right after they came out of the oven. Well, my cousin went over and grabbed a piping-hot cookie. When he found out how hot it was, he started screaming, and his solution was to shove the whole thing in his mouth at once. This same cousin took our 97-year-old great-grandfather's cane away from him and hit him over the head with it. This kid was an absolute menace, and no one could stand being around him.

My parents were good disciplinarians, and when my father said do something, you did it. My aunt and uncle were going out of town, and they asked my parents, "Will you take care of our son?" My parents said, "Absolutely!" Shortly after, my cousin came running in the house, acting as foolish as ever. My dad said, "Come here," and then he very calmly said, "Here are the rules. I want you to do this, this, and this. If you don't do it, this is what will happen." It was only seconds before the first rule was broken. My dad disciplined him right there on the spot.

For those days that his parents were gone, my cousin was a perfect gentleman. He never talked back to anyone. He was totally transformed in the presence of my father, and he was really an enjoyable person to be around. We even discovered he had a fun personality!

When his parents returned, my cousin was standing at the front door of our house. He ran out the door, yelling, "M.L. spanked me!" In that instant of time, he went right back to his old nature. Do you know why? Because his parents wouldn't discipline him. They would warn him and warn him and warn him and warn him, but they never took action on any of their threats.

If you want obedient, well-mannered children, you must discipline with consistency. Say to them, "Here's the rule. If you do this, this is what I'm going to do. If you don't do this, this is what I'm going to do." Then follow through every time.

If you want obedient, well-mannered children, you must discipline with consistency.

Tell your child to do something in a calm, loving tone. Don't ever beg or plead, because if you do that, here's what could happen. Imagine your son Grayson is riding his bicycle out into the street. You see a car coming and yell, "Grayson, stop!" But Grayson is so used to your begging and pleading that he says to himself, *I don't have to listen. My parent hasn't said it 13 times yet.* So he keeps going on out into the road, and you can't get to him in time.

You must train your children, "When you hear me say something, you respond right now, and if you don't, there will be consequences." If you do not train your child to respond to your voice the first time, you're not training your children in the ways of God. God will not plead with your child. He will tell your child one time, and if they don't do it, they will experience the consequences.

Look at our society today. God loves America very much, but we are paying a high price because of our rebellion against God, and so are our children. God is not sitting up in heaven saying, "Oh, please, America, don't do that." He's saying, "I'm telling you to stop, and if you don't, you're going to suffer the penalty every time you do it." When God says something, He means it. Your children need to learn that early in life.

21

Discipline Strategies, Part 2

CORRECTION

This "how to" of correction is undoubtedly the most controversial part of discipline. This is an area in which the devil has deceived our society, and our children are paying a terrible price. Humanistic teachings have duped people into believing discipline is harmful and unneeded. A self-indulgent and rebellious society has grown out of such lies. Today's children feel unloved and lack the discipline needed to be successful in any area of their lives. Parents, you must settle this fact right now: God is a disciplinarian, and He expects you to discipline your children according to His Word.

God is a disciplinarian, and He expects you to discipline your children according to His Word.

To help you learn how to discipline God's way, we're going to talk about the dos and don'ts of discipline. We've already talked about spanking. The good thing about spanking, especially with young children, is that it's efficient. It's over and done with quickly. Little kids don't hold a grudge, but they remember the pain and learn how to avoid it the next time.

A parent's hands are meant to comfort and to express love. Therefore, it is best to use a small wooden spoon or some type of paddle that will sting but not cause harm to the child. It is wrong to grab a child and start flailing him, striking him all over the body wherever the blows land. Maybe you were disciplined that way—your mom or dad would get mad and start yelling and name-calling and then grab you and start flailing you. If that is what is in the archives of your past, don't repeat that pattern with your own children. The proper message you want to give to your child when you are disciplining is, "I am not out of control, and I don't hate you. You've done something that violated my rules. I'm going to discipline you in a very controlled way, but I love you and forgive you."

Another option is grounding. There are times when you may need to ground a child for their own protection, but it's a long-term discipline that affects the entire family. Make sure the length of time for the grounding is reasonable and fitting for the circumstances. Then be consistent with enforcing it. Extra chores, loss of privileges, having to repent to someone, or making restitution are all in the bag of choices when you're looking for ways to discipline your child. Spanking is not the answer to everything, especially as children get older. We (Jimmy and Karen) spanked our children until they hit puberty, and then we used other discipline options.

Never resort to name-calling. When you call a child "idiot," "stupid," "clumsy," or any other such name, you are speaking a curse on them. I (Jimmy) knew someone whose pet name for their child was "Stupid." They called him that all the time and thought it would have the effect of reverse psychology. This child was sniffing glue in the eighth grade and became brain damaged as a result. You must speak life and encouragement to your children at all times, even when disciplining.

Never discipline a child in public. Discipline is a private matter and should be done one-on-one between the parent and that child alone. It shames them when it is done in front of others. If your child starts doing something in public, warn them, and if they continue, immediately get up and take them to a private place to discipline them. Don't let them call your bluff on it. Discipline your children for public behavior but do it in a private way.

One time we were at a restaurant, and my (Jimmy's) parents were with us. Brent was flicking macaroni noodles at Julie. I looked over at him and said, "Don't do that, Brent." He hadn't learned that he couldn't call my bluff in public, and he continued his antics. I smiled across the table and said, "Brent, let's go to the car." He replied, "Huh?" I took Brent out to the car and spanked him.

At that point in our lives, Karen and I carried a little wooden paddle with us everywhere we went. And we had it with us one day when we were getting a family picture taken. Julie and Brent were having one of their perpetual fights, goading and picking at each other. We were trying to get a nice family picture taken, but it's hard to look pleasant when one of your children is provoking you and ruining an important moment. Brent was harassing and elbowing Julie while the photographer was trying to frame us up for the picture. I said, "Brent, stop." He looked back at me and just kind of smiled one of those mischievous smiles like, **I know you're not going to spank me here getting a picture taken.** He kept it up, and I said to the photographer, "Do you have a private room that we could borrow for a moment?" The photographer said, "Excuse me?" I said, "Is anyone using that room over there?" He said, "No."

I leaned over to Karen and said, "Let me see the spoon." She pulled it out of her purse, and I took Brent into that room. I said, "Now I told you not to do that," and I spanked him. Afterward, I dried his tears and took him back to his place beside Julie. When I sat down in my place, the photographer stepped away from his camera, walked up, and said, "Sir, for 25 years I have been putting up with children. Thank you!" I thought he was going to cry!

If your children start doing something in public, don't start calling them names or grabbing at them or flailing them. Publicly shaming your child is never godly discipline. (And in today's culture, you might end up being arrested!)

Never yell at your child. I (Karen) will be the first to tell you that I broke this rule at times when the kids were young. It can be so hard not to raise your voice at your kids! But when you are firm and consistent, a raised volume isn't necessary in the discipline process.

Yelling is a good indication you are not in control of your emotions, and that spells caution. Do you know why people abuse their children? Often, it's because they wait until their emotions are out of control before they take action. I'm so grateful for Jimmy because whenever our children disobeyed, he did something about it right then while his emotions were under control. And whenever I did yell, I was quick to apologize and make it right.

Yelling is a good indication you are not in control of your emotions.

Never resort to extreme consequences. An example would be a parent who says, "You didn't clean your room, so go sleep out in the backyard." That is extremism. Use common sense and be cautious about dipping back into your past. Just because your parents did it doesn't mean it is right. Years ago, there was a couple in our church who believed you should spank a child until you broke the rebellion in that child's spirit. That's an extremely dangerous way to spank a child, and we have never found any biblical documentation for such a philosophy. And by the way, these people did bruise and injure their children, and they were turned in to the authorities because of it.

To be clear, we do not believe in, support, or promote excessive spanking. Two or three swats is sufficient. Plus, there comes a time when you discover spanking isn't the most effective discipline anymore. Taking away privileges or doing extra chores is more painful to an older child than a couple of swats with the paddle.

Once again, let's go over the steps in the correct way to spank a child:

1. Communicate clearly what the child did wrong.
2. Take them to a private place.

3. Swat the child two or three times on their bottom with an appropriate type of paddle.

4. Give hugs and comfort.

5. Forgive them and pray for them.

Compassion

The most important factor that enables you to hold your children's behavior in check is the relationship you have with them. The balance of love (or grace) and truth is critical in maintaining a relationship with your children. If you raise your children with an equal emphasis on your relationship with them and the rules you expect them to obey, you will be able to produce the results you desire—wholesome, healthy-minded young people.

When Brent was about 15 years old, I (Jimmy) felt like I was losing him. Because he was doing some foolish things, I felt like I needed to tighten the reins on him and help him become a man. I kept disciplining him and doing what I felt like was right, but I also felt like Brent was turning his heart away from me.

One day, I went to him and said, "Brent, let's go play golf somewhere." He looked rather surprised and asked, "Just me and you?"

"Yes, just you and me. Where do you want to go?"

"You mean, like Amarillo?"

"No, outside of Amarillo. We're going to go somewhere."

"Really?"

"Yeah. Where do you want to go?"

"Well, where can we go?"

"You want to go to Phoenix?"

"Phoenix, Arizona?"

"Yes, Phoenix, Arizona."

"Just me and you?"

"That's right."

With a typical 15-year-old's mindset, Brent asked, "Can I get out of school?" "Yes, you can get out of school." He got out of school, and we flew to Phoenix.

When we arrived, I said, "What kind of car do you want to rent?" He asked, "Are you going to let me drive?" I replied, "No, but you can pick the car." Brent chose a convertible, and we put the top down. That night, the Phoenix Suns were playing basketball, and he said, "Oh, Dad, I want to go see the Phoenix Suns." So we got tickets and went to the game. They played the Portland Trailblazers, and it was a great game.

We played golf the next day and the following day. It was a good time together. The second day we were sitting in the golf cart waiting for the people in front of us to play, and Brent looked over at me and asked, "Why are you being so hard on me?" I replied, "Because I love you." Brent said, "Dad, I'm not stupid. You don't have to worry about me." I responded, "Brent, I know you're not stupid, but I am concerned about you, about what's going on with you and all the people around you, about all the things you have an opportunity to do right now that I know are tempting to you. I'm not trying to be mean to you, Brent. I'm just trying to do the right thing as a father." Brent said, "Dad, you just need to understand I'm growing up, and I need to make some of my own choices." I said, "Brent, you just need to understand that scares me. It scares me the choices that you're able to make right now. I'm not trying to hurt you. I'm trying to protect you."

It took two days of having fun with my son before his heart opened up to me. When you lose your child's heart, you lose them. If they don't know that you love them, you can't influence their lives, and at some point, they become bitter and rebellious.

Throughout the years when our kids were growing up, one of the most important gauges we watched was, "Do we have their hearts? Are we still having fun together? Can we still talk?" Even when we were disciplining them and going through hard times, we always wanted to have good relationships with them. I realized during that Phoenix trip how close I came to losing Brent. He was drawing away, and I was busy. I am so glad I pursued him and didn't let him get away, because it was a critical time in his life.

When you feel your children pulling away from you, run after them. It's easy in this troubled, violent world to worry so much about everything having to do with your children that you smother their hope and their joy for living. That's why you must keep the light of Jesus shining in your life at all times and balance rules with love. As you guide, direct, and discipline your children, never let them lose sight of your compassion and love modeled after your heavenly Father. Love gives you the right to discipline even when their behavior is communicating something else. Their relationship with you and their heavenly Father is more important than anything else. Without it, rebellion is bound to be the result.

When you feel your children pulling away from you, run after them.

When Brent was going through that difficult stage, I (Karen) was so worried about him. I kept praying, "Lord, I just need for You to help us." One day, the Lord spoke clearly to my heart and asked me, "When are you going to start trusting Me?" It was the most beautiful, freeing moment. If we are going to ask the Lord to help us raise our kids the right way, we must believe that He is listening and that He knows what we and our children need.

22

Shameless Sexuality

We've arrived at the topic that many parents try to avoid as long as possible. Some parents are uncomfortable because they don't know what to say, and others are afraid to say anything because their personal experience involves so much shame. Meanwhile, children are finding out about it from friends, social media, TV shows, music videos, etc. In the fight for the souls of our children, this subject is a serious battle because it's a core part of our human identity that the enemy wants to steal and corrupt. Parents desperately need to understand the truth of what God's Word says about this topic and teach it to their children with age-appropriate language and explanations. So buckle up, Moms and Dads—it's time to talk about sex.

In a series of surveys and focus groups, Be Broken Ministry asked parents, "Why do you not talk with your children about sex?" Here are some of the most common answers:

- I'm afraid I will make my child uncomfortable.
- I'm afraid I will ruin my child's innocence.
- My child isn't old enough to need to know about sex.
- My kid would never be interested in pornography.
- I'm afraid my child might find out about my own past.[1]

Some parents are under the false impression that if they don't talk about something, it will go away, but that's just not true when it comes to sex. Children will find out about it one way or another. Wouldn't you rather them know what God says about sex? Of course, that means you need to know what God says about sex (and sexuality in general) in order to share that with your children.

The Origin of Sexuality

Would it surprise you to know that your sexuality comes from God? Well, it does! Genesis 1:27 says,

Your sexuality comes from God.

> So God created mankind in his own image,
>   in the image of God he created them;
>   male and female he created them (NIV).

Three times in this short text, the word "create" is used to highlight God's handiwork. Man reflects God's glory in his masculinity, just as woman reflects God in her femininity. Males and females are equal, but we are not interchangeable.

Gender

We recognize saying there are only two genders—male and female—is a radical statement in today's world. In February 2022, Healthline.com published an article titled, "68 Terms That Describe Gender Identity and Expression." A year later, in February 2023, SexualDiversity.org offered a list of 94 gender identities. And according to *Medical News Today*, "There is no fixed number of gender identities. They occur on a spectrum, which really means that the possibilities are infinite."[2]

There is no differentiation in Scripture between gender identity and biological sex. They are one and the same. Men are male, and women are female. There's no spectrum, even though "human rights" activists desperately try to find it. Instead, Jesus points back to Genesis: "Have you not read that He who made them at the beginning 'made them male and female,' and said, 'For this reason a man shall leave his father and mother and be joined to his wife, and the two shall become one flesh'?" (Matthew 19:4).

We realize that people will probably accuse of us being "cissexists" (discriminating and excluding transgender and nonbinary individuals). And yes, some people truly feel confused about their identity. They honestly believe that their physical makeup doesn't match their psychological makeup, and they are hurting. Just like everyone else, these people deserve our love, respect, and compassion. We should never abuse, harass, or mock someone who is struggling to find the truth.

However, the answer is not self-mutilation. The fact is that you cannot change or reassign your gender. Removing or altering genitalia does not result in reassigning a person from male to female or female to male. Any gender change is in name only.

The thought behind gender reassignment is that humans are simply biological accidents, and gender is socially constructed. If a person feels he or she has been given the wrong gender assignment, medical procedures can correct the "error." To hold such a position a person must believe either that there is no God, or He exists but is a bungling idiot, much the same way an absent-minded scientist would create a disaster by mixing the wrong chemicals. The Bible, however, presents God in a different light.

For You formed my inward parts;
You covered me in my mother's womb.
I will praise You, for I am fearfully *and* wonderfully made;
Marvelous are Your works,
And *that* my soul knows very well.
My frame was not hidden from You,

When I was made in secret,
And skillfully wrought in the lowest parts of the earth.
Your eyes saw my substance, being yet unformed.
And in Your book they all were written,
The days fashioned for me,
When *as yet there were* none of them.
How precious also are Your thoughts to me, O God!
How great is the sum of them!
If I should count them, they would be more in number than the sand;
When I awake, I am still with You (Psalm 139:13–18).

If we are fearfully and wonderfully made by God, and He doesn't make mistakes, then why would people assume they have been assigned the wrong gender? Gender is not a social construct—it's a *God* construct.

Gender is not a social construct—it's a *God* construct.

Author and public speaker Walt Heyer grew up with tremendous confusion about his gender identity. As an adult, he had gender reassignment surgery and lived as a transgender female for eight years. Walt writes, "No matter how feminine I appeared, like all transgenders, I was just a man in a dress. I was unhappy, regretful of having transitioned, and I attempted suicide. Gender surgery is not effective treatment for depression, anxiety or mental disorders."[3] Having now been de-transitioned (returned to male) for more than 30 years, Walt works to help others through the de-transition process through his website, SexChangeRegret.com.

The world is telling our children, "Be true to your authentic self!" What they really mean is do what you want when you want and however you want because there are no rules. But when you are a follower of Jesus Christ, you give up the right of self-determination in any area of your life, and that includes your sexuality.

Dr. Kevin DeYoung of The Gospel Coalition writes, "We do not have an inalienable right to do whatever we want with our physical selves. We belong to God and should glorify him with our bodies."[4] The apostle Paul agreed:

> I beseech you therefore, brethren, by the mercies of God, that you present your bodies a living sacrifice, holy, acceptable to God, *which is* your reasonable service. And do not be conformed to this world, but be transformed by the renewing of your mind, that you may prove what *is* that good and acceptable and perfect will of God (Romans 12:1–2).

Christians have the responsibility to stand firm on the truth of God's Word while demonstrating His love. In this way they live out the commandment to love God and love people (in that particular order). The devil is attacking people with gender confusion to the point that they don't know where to turn or what to do. God has given us the assignment to lead people to the truth and to take authority over the devil and his lies (see Luke 10:19).

Sex

When God created Adam and Eve, they "were both naked, and they felt no shame" (Genesis 2:25 NIV). There were no bathrobes hanging on a nearby tree for the first man and woman, because there was no need to cover up. Instead, "a man leaves his father and mother and is united to his wife, and they become one flesh" (v. 24 NIV). God created sex for two main reasons: to expand the human race (God's family) and for pleasure in marriage.

Sexuality is central to God's purpose for your life. You're a sexual person, and even though you may never have realized it, your child is a sexual person. God is the One who created us that way. The reason why Satan attacks sexuality so strongly is that he understands it is a part of God's creation of us. And if he can get us to fall sexually, then we will never be able to accomplish God's purpose for our lives.

Sexuality and the Fall

Look how many times the issue of sexuality is mentioned in the fall of mankind.

> So when the woman saw that the tree *was* good for food, that it *was* pleasant to the eyes, and a tree desirable to make *one* wise, she took of its fruit and ate. She also gave to her husband with her, and he ate. Then the eyes of both of them were open and they knew that they *were* naked; and they sewed fig leaves together and made themselves coverings (Genesis 3:6–7).

The very first sign of the fall of mankind was shame related to sexuality. Adam and Eve sewed fig leaves together and hid their sexual parts (their genitals) from God and from each other.

> And they heard the sound of the LORD God walking in the garden in the cool of the day, and Adam and his wife hid themselves from the presence of the LORD God among the trees of the garden. Then the LORD God called to Adam and said to him, "Where *are* you?" And he said, "I heard Your voice in the garden, and I was afraid because I was naked" (Genesis 3:8–10).

A common belief is that Adam was hiding from God because he had sinned. But that is not true. Obviously, Adam knew he was naked after he sinned, but when God asked, "Where are you?" (or "Why are you hiding from me?") Adam says, "I was afraid because I was naked." In Adam's mind the reason he needed to hide from God is because he was ashamed of his God-given sexuality. Remember, God created Adam and Eve naked without shame. Satan wants us to be ashamed of our God-given sexuality so that we will hide it from God.

> And He said, "Who told you that you *were* naked? Have you eaten from the tree of which I commanded you that you should not eat?" (Genesis 3:11).

God was not asking these questions because He did not know the answers. Rather, He was asking for Adam's purpose and for our purpose. In essence, God was saying to Adam, "Someone must have told you that there was something wrong with your sexuality. That could not have come from me. If you are hiding yourself behind these fig leaves, someone has been messing with you."

God knew the shame had come from Satan, but Adam probably didn't. That's the nature of the enemy—he stealthily comes in like a serpent, and we believe the things he tells us without even realizing he is the one who told us. That is one reason why people in today's world are so sexually deceived today. They don't believe the devil told them anything but rather that they are "enlightened" and the "right" thing to do is really the wrong thing. They have been listening to the devil's whispers without knowing it.

The purpose of this chapter is not to make you feel bad about anything you have done. It is to help you understand how you can overcome the devil's attempts to conquer you and your children's sexuality. In Genesis chapter 3, Adam and Eve fell, and the devil began to educate them in his deceptive way about sex. By Genesis chapter 6, the entire world had been sexually corrupted.

> Then the LORD saw that the wickedness of man *was* great in the earth, and *that* every intent of the thoughts of his heart *was* only evil continually. And the LORD was sorry that He had made man on the earth, and He was grieved in His heart. So the LORD said, "I will destroy man whom I have created from the face of the earth, both man and beast, creeping thing and birds of the air, for I am sorry that I have made them." But Noah found grace in the eyes of the LORD. This is the

genealogy of Noah. Noah was a just man, perfect in his generations. Noah walked with God. And Noah begot three sons: Shem, Ham, and Japheth. The earth also was corrupt before God, and the earth was filled with violence. So God looked upon the earth, and indeed it was corrupt; for all flesh had corrupted their way on the earth (vv. 5–12).

That word corrupt means morally perverted and sexually immoral. That kind of sounds like our world today, doesn't it?

God looked down and regretted that He had ever made man on the earth. The reason He regretted His creation was this: when Satan controls the world sexually, the world cannot accomplish the purposes of God. God has a purpose in our lives, and sexuality is central to that purpose.

When Satan controls the world sexually, the world cannot accomplish the purposes of God.

Some people get a little grossed out when they hear talk about God and sex. But God is the one who created it, and He said it was very good. When God sees us having sex in the confines of marriage, He loves that. Again, people get uncomfortable when you say God loves to see people having sex, but He does. It's not as if He doesn't know it's happening, by the way. God is everywhere, even in your bedroom, and sex isn't gross to Him.

The shame of sexuality is a result of the fall. When you feel any twinge of shame about your God-given sexuality, that is from the enemy. Romans 8:1 says, "There is now no condemnation for those who are in Christ Jesus" (NIV). When we sin sexually, there is righteous guilt and conviction, but shame is never from God. God will never make you feel ashamed of being sexually aroused. A desire for sex isn't wrong because He created you with that desire. And He isn't afraid of the language surrounding sex, such as "pleasure" and "orgasm."

From the very beginning, Satan has attacked our sexuality and tried to shame us for it because he understands that whoever controls our sexuality controls us. And if the enemy controls you, you can no longer fulfill your purpose for God.

Teaching Our Children

When Brent was about 10 years old, we were eating dinner as a family one night, and he said, "Mom and Dad, what does *blank* mean?" (But instead of *blank*, he said the worst curse word you can think of). Julie dropped her fork! I (Jimmy) asked where he had heard that word, and he said it was written on a building in the park where he was playing that day. I answered, "Well, it means sex, which is something that married couples do." (I figured that was all his little five-year-old mind could handle). Brent responded, "Yeah, that's what my friend told me." I thought, *Oh, no!*

You should always do your best to protect your children from ungodly influences, but the fact is that there will be times when your children see and hear things you don't want them to see and hear. The way you choose to respond will be incredibly instrumental in the way they view not only that topic but also themselves. Do you panic and yell and lecture? Or do you remain calm and composed as you discuss the situation?

You don't need to have the full "birds and bees" conversation with your toddler. That would be too much "big" information for a "little" mind. Rather, sexuality should be a series of ongoing, age-appropriate conversations. But even when children are very young, you can teach them the correct names of their private body parts. Boys have a penis, scrotum, and testicles. Girls have a vulva, vagina, and breasts. Teach your child about body privacy and how we don't let anyone see or touch our private parts (unless it's a trusted adult in an appropriate setting, like a doctor).

Did you know that today's children are beginning to go through puberty earlier than previous generations? In fact, early puberty ("precocious puberty") is only considered to occur in girls seven years or younger and in boys eight years or younger. This means parents can no longer wait until their children are teenagers to explain the physical and emotional changes that will be happening. Girls as young as eight need to know about breast development and menstrual cycles. Boys as young as nine need to know about erections. Both genders need to understand the function and purpose of their body parts, and they need their parents' reassurance that changes are a normal part of growing up. (And if any changes are happening that aren't normal, your child needs your help and guidance even more.)

You are the most trustworthy person to talk to your children about sex, and your children need to know that they can ask you anything. Yes, *anything.* Christian mom and author Mandy Majors was shocked when her fourth-grade daughter asked her a very sexually explicit question based on something a young friend had told the daughter about. Naturally, Mandy was angry and grieved at the loss of her daughter's innocence. As a young mom, she wasn't ready to have that kind of conversation! But as a believer, Mandy went to the Lord and asked for His help. She discovered that these awkward conversations are actually a gift and a way to live out Deuteronomy 6:6–7:

> These commandments that I give you today are to be on your hearts. Impress them on your children. Talk about them when you sit at home and when you walk along the road, when you lie down and when you get up (NIV).

Mandy shares, "The solution was so simple, and it was right there in my Bible: *open communication. It was about having healthy, on-the-go conversations with my kids about the everyday issues and questions they struggle with.*"[5]

Don't make your child search the internet for information. Because they will if they think it's their only option. Do you want your child learning about masturbation, oral and anal sex, or threesomes from strangers online? (We realize you would rather your children not learn about those things at all, at least until they're adults, but in today's world, that's just not probable.) We love Mandy's advice to parents:

Don't make your child search the internet for information.

Be your child's Google. Continually tell your kids, "Not everything you hear on the playground or read online is true. When you're curious about something or heard a new word you don't understand, ask me. Never search online."

If your child asks a question you don't know the answer to or if you aren't sure how to answer the question in age-appropriate terms, buy some time to find the answer or figure out how much to share. Here are a few ways you can do that:

- It's perfectly okay to say, "Can I have a day to pray about this? I want to give you the right information." My personal rule is to get back to my kids in twenty-four hours. This shows them that their questions matter.

- You could also say, "We need to cover a few other things before we talk about this topic." For example, before defining oral and anal sex, set a foundation for that conversation by telling your child how babies are formed (i.e., egg and sperm). Kids today are often exposed to more advanced sexual topics at much younger ages, which means we need to start the first sex talk earlier. These talks will become ongoing discussions that will get more detailed as your kids get older.

- If your child's question includes a slang word, and you don't know what it means, tell your child that you need to do some research first. Then Google the word later (but not in front of your child). Use technology to your advantage....

Make a point of acknowledging that your kids' curiosity is natural, and you're their go-to source for information.

Every question your child asks is an opportunity to build more open communication in your home. Take advantage of it![6]

A man in his fifties once told me (Jimmy), "I struggled with pornography all my life. The other day my son was going to college, and I saw him loading up his computer. I sat him down and said, 'Son, I want you to listen to me. I have struggled with pornography all my life, and I do not want you to follow in my footsteps. I want you to make me a promise that that computer of yours will not be used for pornography. And every time you are tempted you will call me on the phone, and we will talk and pray together." His son said, "Daddy, I promise." And that began an ongoing conversation. I looked at this man and said, "You are a smart man. You have kept your son from so many problems by having a daddy that he can call and talk to about those kinds of issues."

23

Lies About Sex, Part 1

There is no doubt about it—the sex educator of today's society is Satan. The Bible is being scorned and rejected more than ever before as the basis of authority, and even believers are accepting many lies as truth. Here are a few that every godly parent needs to be aware of.

Lie #1: Only vaginal intercourse counts as "sex."

There is a common belief today among youth and some adults that only vaginal penetration with a penis is sex. People say, "It's not sex if we just pet or masturbate each other or if we have oral sex." However, in Matthew 5:28, Jesus says, "Anyone who looks at a woman lustfully has already committed adultery with her in his heart" (NIV). It does not have to be physical to be sex in God's sight.

In 1 Corinthians 6:19, we are told that our bodies are the temple of the Holy Spirit. In the Temple in Israel there were four parts. The outer court, called the Court of the Gentiles, was where anyone could go. Then there was the inner court, where only priests could go. Next was the Holy Place, where only a few priests could go. And finally, there was the Holy of Holies, where only the high priest could go.

There is a direct correlation between our bodies and the four different places in the Temple. Our bodies have an outer court, which is our hands and forearms. If you want to walk up and shake someone's hand or touch their arm, that is appropriate and acceptable in American culture.

Then there are the inner court areas, such as your chest, back, and face. It would not be acceptable for a stranger to walk up to you and touch your face or rub your back. But when you see a close friend or relative, it would be normal to hug and pat each other on the back and perhaps touch cheek to cheek.

The Holy Place areas of your body are your bottom and your lips. You may only kiss a few people, such as your mother, and very few people should have access to your bottom. It would be inappropriate for some random person to walk by casually and pat you on your rear end.

Finally, the Holy of Holies area is your genitals. Only one person can go there—your spouse. If anyone other than your spouse touches you in a sexual way in your genitals, that is sex, and that is sin.

Lie #2: Sex is the best way to express love.

Many young people pride themselves on not having sex on the first date or with a casual stranger. They say, "If I'm going to have sex with someone, I have to love them first."

As a young man, I (Jimmy) was immoral. I am not proud of this at all, but I told a lot of girls that I loved them in order to get something from them, and many of my friends did the same thing. If you have a daughter, you need to tell them this truth: you never know if a boy loves you until he is standing in front of a preacher, putting a wedding ring on your finger, and committing the rest of his life to you in the presence of God.

There are plenty of boys who tell girls, "If you love me, you will let me do this or that." Teach your daughter to say, "If you loved me, you would not put me in that position. You would not force me to have sex or threaten to abandon me." Any boy who would force a girl to have sex to stay in the relationship is not a boy worth keeping. He is not the kind of man you want to marry.

Love is not enough of a reason to have sex with someone, especially because it could just be infatuation, or "puppy love," as we used to call it. It is not real love until there is a lifelong commitment behind it. Love is not demonstrated in what you are demanding from a person; it is demonstrated in what you are willing to *give* to a person. When a person is demanding something from you, they are not showing true love.

When a person is demanding something from you, they are not showing true love.

Your children also need to know this: whomever they are dating right now is probably not the person they are going to marry. Sure, it's possible that this guy or this girl is the "one," but it is probably someone else. Your children are likely dating someone else's wife or husband, so they need to treat them with respect and honor. Don't use them up like a piece of furniture or a car and then trade them out for a newer model. It is wrong to have sex with someone, even if you think you might love them, if that love has not been demonstrated in a marriage covenant.

Lie #3: Experience makes you a better lover.

Many people believe that the more sexually experienced you are before marriage, the better lover you will be once you get married. However, research has proven that the most sexually satisfied people in marriage are the least sexual before they get married.[1] If you have had a lot of sex before you get married, typically the only "extra" thing you have going into marriage is heartache.

People who have had a lot of sex before marriage often have a fear of intimacy—they have difficulty opening up and being truly intimate (emotionally and spiritually). They may also have sub-par relationship skills, because rather than talking and learning to deal with problems in the relationship, they had sex. Sex feels good in the moment, but it can make you a lazy partner.

Lie #4: Sex deepens your intimacy before marriage.

How can you know if you and your partner are really meant for each other? Many people think the answer is to have sex. More than half of people getting married today have lived together before marriage.[2] In other words, they have had sex before marriage. The reason why many women cohabitate before marriage is they want to keep the man from leaving and hopefully lead the relationship to marriage. The reason why many men cohabitate before marriage is so they can have the conveniences of marriage, including sex, without a commitment. Research continually shows that people who cohabitate before marriage have a higher divorce rate than people who do not.[3]

The spirit of covenant marriage says this: "I am giving away rights, and I am sacrificially assuming responsibility until death. I am committing the rest of my life to you. It's all about you. I am going to serve you, and I am going to cherish you. I am going to take care of you regardless of sickness, poverty, or difficulty. I am going to serve and love you for the rest of my life."

Meanwhile, the spirit of cohabitation and sex before marriage says this: "I am going to see how good you are at taking care of me, and if you are good enough, I will marry you. But if you do not keep it up, I will divorce you. It's all about me, and this is a tryout."

Do you want that second kind of relationship? We don't either. One thing we love about God is that He promises in His Word, "Never will I leave you; never will I forsake you" (Hebrews 13:5 NIV). We do not serve a God who makes us perform to keep His favor. Instead, He comes to us and says, "On your worst day, I am still your best friend. I am going to be here. I am committed to this relationship forever and ever."

The purpose of dating is not to see how good you are in bed. The purpose of dating is to see how good your character is and to make sure you are *spiritually* compatible. The greatest intimacy in the world is created by a relationship with the Lord Jesus Christ. And when two people know and love God and know and love each other, sex is phenomenal. But when you have two people who are immature and do not know how to deal with issues and think that sex is intimacy, they have no real, lasting bond. It is one of the greatest deceptions in the whole world.

Lie #5: Pornography doesn't hurt anyone.

When I (Jimmy) was about 11 years old, I was introduced to pornography. A neighbor had access to *Playboy* magazines, and every month a group of us boys would gather to look at the new one. Some of the older boys even showed the younger ones how to masturbate.

As I got older, *Playboy* seemed mild compared to many of the things I saw, especially in college. At one party I attended, an XXX-rated film was shown. Not only was I aroused, but I was also fascinated by the women in it. They were sexually aggressive and totally uninhibited. This film fixed in my mind a deep deception about women and sex that had a very negative impact on my marriage in our early years.

Today, pornography is more readily accessible than ever—just a few taps or clicks away on a computer, tablet, or cell phone. One internet porn giant receives 3.2 billion visits per month (more than Amazon or Netflix).[4] The porn industry is extremely profitable, with global revenue reaching $100 billion.[5] And it's not just a boy issue. An in-depth study by Josh McDowell and the Barna Group found that "56 percent of women 25 years and under seek out porn, and one-third seek it out monthly."[6]

There is a massive cultural push to embrace pornography as a normal and even beneficial part of our sexuality. However, this is a complete lie from the enemy. Pornography isn't about nakedness, beautiful men and women, or sex. It is a multilayered system of Satanic deception that refutes God's Word and His will concerning the sacred nature of sex, the character of God, the role of men and women, the marriage covenant, love, and human fulfillment. Until we realize what pornography is really about and attack the thought system behind it, we will never be free.

Until we realize what pornography is really about and attack the thought system behind it, we will never be free.

We could fill an entire book with the problems of pornography, but here are a few to consider:

The people in pornography are often explicitly presented as objects, and porn videos are listed and labeled with the specific acts they perform or physical attributes they possess so the observer can "order" porn that fits their exact expectations. With so many people consuming pornography, is it any wonder that many are developing attitudes of sexual entitlement and objectification? Reducing people to physical terms and self-serving labels is the exact type of sexual objectification that sets the stage for sexual violence.[7]

In fact, research routinely shows that frequent porn consumers are more likely to sexually objectify and dehumanize others,[8] more likely to express an intent to rape,[9] less likely to intervene during a sexual assault,[10] more likely to victim-blame survivors of sexual violence,[11] more likely to support violence against women,[12] more likely to forward sexts without consent,[13] and more likely to commit actual acts of sexual violence.[14]

Lie #6: Parents shouldn't talk to their kids about masturbation.

If there's anything more awkward for parents than talking to their kids about sex, it's talking to their kids about masturbation. Yes, it's the dreaded m-word. Masturbation is "the stimulation or manipulation of one's own genitals, especially to orgasm; sexual self-gratification."[15] While it can also refer to non-intercourse activity with a partner, self-pleasure is most often the definition we think of for this word.

Some parents don't acknowledge masturbation at all because they assume it will be a non-issue. "My child would *never* do that." Others are afraid to mention it, and they hope that by ignoring it, it will go away. This is the same approach many parents take to pornography. The problem is that like pornography, masturbation doesn't suddenly cease to exist just because we aren't comfortable talking about it. And, of course, there are parents who are addicted to pornography or masturbation themselves.

Our children need us to talk to them about *all* aspects of sexuality, and yes, that includes masturbation. But what do we even say about this topic? It seems so taboo, especially within Christianity, but there's no verse in the Bible specifically forbidding it. In fact, the word "masturbation" isn't in the Bible at all. So does that mean it's totally fine? Or is it a sin that makes a person dirty and gross?

In her book *TALK*, Mandy Majors examines four possible approaches for talking to your child about masturbation:

1. "It's natural. Do it."
2. "It's wrong. Don't do it."
3. "It's not something that should be a habit, but it may happen."
4. We can stay silent on the issue and let our kids figure it out for themselves.[16]

Let's start by crossing the fourth approach off the list. As parents, we are the God-given experts for our children, and it's our responsibility to teach them about life. (And if we don't know about something, we need to educate ourselves.) Let's look at the remaining three options.

It's natural. Do It.

Majors writes, "God designed our bodies with the capacity to feel pleasure when our genitals are stimulated. So we should never shame our kids or give them the impression that the bodies God gave them are somehow dirty or sinful. Never! Instead, we should encourage [them] that the changes they are experiencing are completely natural."[17] Children are going to explore their bodies, just as you most likely did at that age. This curiosity isn't bad or wrong, and neither is feeling sexual pleasure.

It's wrong. Don't do it.

There are many people who believe masturbation is completely sinful and immoral. There are even old wives' tales, like, "If you touch yourself, your hand will fall off." Obviously, that's not going to physically happen, but masturbation can be addicting when it's connected with pornography or sexual intercourse outside of marriage. The Bible is clear in 1 Corinthians 6:18 that we should "flee sexual immorality." As children of God, we shouldn't be a slave to anything, including our sexual desires. So even though this can be a gray area for believers, if masturbation leads to any kind of addiction, then the answer should be no.

As children of God, we shouldn't be a slave to anything, including our sexual desires.

It's not something that should be a habit, but it may happen.

Majors writes, "We need to be real and honest with our kids about masturbation. A safe place where they can talk about it openly, without shame or fear over how we'll respond."[18] This is true for parents of sons *and* parents of daughters. Girls should not be shamed for their sexuality any more than boys should be given a free pass for immorality. Society tends to label masturbation as a "guy" thing, but the truth is that both genders have sexual desires and interests. That's how God made us.

Many children, especially boys, don't discover masturbation through lust or anything like that. Their bodies simply experience a spontaneous sensation without warning or provocation around puberty, usually while sleeping. This is called a "wet dream." Not only is it natural, but it's also involuntary. In other words, they can't help it.

If you shame your children about their thoughts, feelings, and bodies when they are young, they will grow up and bring that shame into their sexual relationship with their spouse. Instead, we need to let our children know that they never have to hide from us. We are always there to listen, to encourage, and to guide.

Talking about masturbation can be uncomfortable or even scary, especially if you have struggled sexually in your past. Before jumping into a conversation with your child, spend some time with the Lord. Confess anything that is weighing on you and ask Him to forgive you. He is so faithful, friends. Not only will He forgive you and release you from that burden, but He will also give you incredible wisdom and insight into the best way to communicate with your child.

By the way, it's totally normal for parents to be mortified even thinking about their kids doing sexual things. Kids feel the same way about their parents having sex! This God-given aversion helps prevent terrible things from happening to healthy-minded people. You don't have to be ashamed about sex to be uncomfortable thinking about your children as sexual beings. But you do have to overcome the aversion, because your God-given responsibility to protect and guide your children must override your discomfort. Keeping them sexually safe prevents more unthinkable things from happening.

24

Lies About Sex, Part 2

Lie #7: Sex without rules is more fun.

Many people think the most fulfilling and exciting sex is outside of marriage, among people who are not encumbered by biblical morality. Research says the opposite:

> The Wheatley report analyzed survey data from 11 countries, including the United States, and its findings suggest that religious "dosage" (the level of a couple's religious involvement) can play a role in reported sexual satisfaction. According to the analysis, *moderately* religious women were 50 percent more likely to report being sexually satisfied in their relationship than women with no religious practice. However, women in *highly* religious relationships (couples who pray together, read scripture at home, and attend church, etc.) were twice as likely as their secular peers to say they were satisfied with their sexual relationship. And the men in these couples were fully four times as likely to report being sexually satisfied as men in relationships with no religious activity.[1]

Another study found that "religion and spirituality have a strong and significant association with sex life satisfaction while controlling for basic sociodemographic variables, and that this relationship is consistent across marital status, age, and gender. The positive association between religion and sexual frequency appeared to be limited to more intrinsic, personal forms such as self-rated spirituality and frequency of prayer."[2]

One of the reasons why sex is better in marriage is there no risk of disease. There is not one disease that is spread by monogamous heterosexual sex. Today, America is a sexual cesspool of diseases. In the 1960s, there were two main sexually transmitted diseases (STDs) in America: gonorrhea and syphilis. Now, according to the World Health Organization in 2022, "more than 30 different bacteria, viruses and parasites are known to be transmitted through sexual contact, including vaginal, anal and oral sex."[3] STDs begin as sexually transmitted infections (STIs) and are only considered a "disease" when symptoms appear.[4] You can have an STI and be entirely asymptomatic, but for STDs, there can be long-term complications, such as pelvic inflammatory disease, infertility, cancer, severe birth defects, and even death.[5] When you have sex outside of marriage, you are taking a huge chance of getting a STI/STD. That really inhibits sexual freedom and expression.

There is not one disease that is spread by monogamous heterosexual sex.

Another reason sex is better in marriage is trust. Rather than having sex with someone who is probably not going to be here a week or a month from now, you are having sex with someone who is committed to you for the rest of your life, in spite of your flaws and problems. Anyone that really believes that the best sex is outside of marriage is just simply not in touch with reality.

Lie #8: God isn't a fan of sex.

Are the boundaries God puts on sex meant to keep us from enjoying it to its fullest? Here are the parameters according to the Bible:

Therefore a man shall leave his father and mother and be joined to his wife, and they shall become one flesh (Genesis 2:24).

The husband should fulfill his marital duty to his wife, and likewise the wife to her husband. The wife does not have authority over her own body but yields it to her husband. In the same way, the husband does not have authority over his own body but yields it to his wife (1 Corinthians 7:3–4 NIV).

According to the Bible, sex belongs to one man (husband) and one woman (woman) in marriage (commitment for life). That's it. Anything else is outside of God's design.

Of all the forces that draw a man and woman together and provide pleasure in their lives, none can surpass sexual intimacy. Designed by God for both pleasure and procreation of the human race, sex is the universally spoken language of love.

However, since mankind's early history, sex also has been one of the most exploited of all our sinful weaknesses. This, combined with the fact that we live in such an immoral, deceived, and seductive society, requires us to be informed and careful as we seek fulfillment in this important area of marriage.

To understand the nature and importance of sexual intimacy, we first must remember that it was God who created this delight in the first place. God wanted us to have pleasure. He also wanted a man and a woman to share a deeply personal area of their lives that would bond them together as it produced intimacy and mutual satisfaction. Therefore, God created sex.

Just as with everything else God has created, Satan has done everything he can to pervert it and use it to destroy us. For this reason, God has told us in His Word how we can fulfill our need for sex while avoiding the sensual destruction everywhere around us.

To understand how to fulfill sexual needs and desires in marriage, while avoiding those areas of sexual involvement God has prohibited in His Word, we first must be aware of what God has commanded us not to do. These are the six sexual practices that God forbids:

1. Sex outside of marriage

   - Adultery is sex when one or both partners are married to someone else.
   - Fornication is sex when both partners are unmarried.

2. Sexual relations with a member of the same sex

   - Traditionally, this is referred to as homosexuality but can also include bisexuality or pansexuality.

3. Sexual relations with a member of your family

   - This is referred to as incest.

4. Sexual relations with minors

   - Traditionally, this has existed under the umbrella term pedophilia but has recently been divided into subcategories: pedophilia (attraction to children generally under 11 years old), hebephilia (attraction to 11–14-year-olds), and ephebophilia (attraction to 15–19 year-olds).

5. Sexual relations with animals

   - Traditionally, this has been referred to as bestiality, but another term is zoophilia.

6. Sexual fantasies or desires for someone other than your spouse

   - This can include lustful fantasies for real or imaginary people and pornography of any kind.

Within the parameters God has placed on sex, we are free to enjoy sex with one another. God is not a prude, and sex is not dirty. The reason He has commanded us not to do these certain things is not because He is trying to keep something good from us. It is because He knows destruction awaits those who practice these things. Therefore, in trusting God and accepting the restrictions He has placed upon our sexual practices, we can enthusiastically pursue sexual fun and fulfillment in marriage.

God is not a prude, and sex is not dirty.

In the glove compartment of your car, you likely have an owner's manual. Have you ever looked at that booklet and thought, *These stupid writers are just trying to control my life. They don't want me to enjoy my car!?* Well, the owner's manual of your life is the Word of God. The God who loves you wrote it, and this is what it says: any sex outside God's design will destroy your life.

Lie #9: The Bible isn't fair.

A common accusation against the Bible is that its sexual standard is unfair to people who are "born a certain way," and it creates prejudice against these people. Let us begin by saying that we live in a fallen world, and we are all born with a sin nature. We all have a disposition to certain sins, and sexual sins are the same before God.

> Do you not know that the unrighteous will not inherit the kingdom of God? Do not be deceived. Neither fornicators, nor idolaters, nor adulterers, nor homosexuals, nor sodomites, nor thieves, nor covetous, nor drunkards, nor revilers, nor extortioners will inherit the kingdom of God (1 Corinthians 6:9–10).

The word "homosexual" in this passage means the one on the giving end of the homosexual act. The word "sodomite" means the one on the receiving end of the homosexual act.

I (Jimmy) was not born with the tendency toward homosexuality, but I do have a tendency toward sexual immorality. No one ever had to teach it to me. Before I got married, I was an immoral person. I looked at pornography and sinned frequently, but I got saved, I repented, and the Lord forgave me of those sins.

Obviously, those are not the only sins I have ever committed, and I have certainly sinned since I got saved. But there is a difference between committing sin and practicing sin. Committing a sin means you do it, but you repent and desire not to do it again. Practicing, on the other hand, means you do it frequently with no intention of stopping. The apostle Paul is not referring to someone who has committed these sexual sins but rather someone who regularly practices them.

We all commit sins because we all are human beings who fall short of God's glory. That's why we need to repent and be forgiven. But practicing a sin means you have no intention of changing. One time I did a marriage seminar, and I met a couple out in the foyer. The wife was as mad as a hornet because her husband had just told her that he had a mistress. Well, this guy was a big man, and he got in my face to tell me, "There is nothing wrong with having a mistress. I need to have my satisfaction!" This man was not committing adultery; he was practicing adultery and trying to justify it. But the Bible clearly says an adulterer will not inherit the kingdom of God.

Have you ever heard the phrase, "Love is love"? It's been a popular hashtag on social media for several years, particularly in the LGBTQ+ community. As of February 2023, 52.8 million Instagram posts include #loveislove. (For anyone who isn't familiar, this phrase means that all forms of love are equally real, valid, and acceptable.) Supporters of this motto believe that sex is a human right, and since all people are created equal, then all human sex is equal too. Therefore, you cannot discriminate against a person's sexual behavior without discriminating against them as a person, and you cannot support a person without condoning their sexual behavior.

Of course, we do not believe those statements are true, and we will explain why. But let's look at a statement from the International Planned Parenthood Federation: "Given that pleasure is an intrinsic aspect of sexuality, the right to seek, express, and determine when to experience it must not be denied to anyone."[6] If we are all sexual beings with the undeniable right to sexual pleasure, then our sexuality becomes the most important part of our identity.

Remember, the true purpose of parenting is to help our children know and love God. As we previously discussed, an integral part of knowing and loving God is finding one's identity in Christ. Satan wants to stop this from happening at any cost. He wants to push our children into finding their identity in anything (and everything) else, and one of his age-old tactics is to elevate sexuality into a god. Instead of surrendering to the Lord, we surrender to our desires. We allow what we think, feel, or want to have more power in our lives than the unwavering truth of Scripture. You may not think that your sexual behavior has anything to do with your worship, but in reality, it has *everything* to do with your worship.

The "sex-positivity" movement tells our children that no one should be able to tell them what to do with their own bodies. They paint parents who teach abstinence for the sake of morality or faith as "sex-negative." One article we read says, "It's a safe bet that unless you're *actively* working to become sex-positive, you're sex-negative."[7] And how can you become sex-positive? You must "genuinely believe that other people can have sex any way they want with whoever they want, so long as consent is involved."[8]

Obviously, according to that definition, the Bible is not sex-positive, and neither is God. Now, many people say they cannot help who they are, and that's true. No one can help who they are. That's why we all need Jesus. He is the only person who can help us. I (Jimmy) was a very dirty young man. I would do terrible things at night and then sing in the church choir the next morning, with absolutely no guilt whatsoever. In fact, I'd be plotting my next escapade. But when I cheated on Karen at my bachelor party one week before our wedding, I realized that I was on the wrong road. I was powerless over my sinful behavior, and in my friend's bathroom I repented of my sins. My life has been dramatically different ever since by the power of God. When someone says they are born that way and they cannot help it, they are exactly right—*they* cannot but God can. He can help anyone.

One argument we've been hearing quite frequently in recent years is that homosexuality isn't actually a sin because Jesus never said anything about it. But let's think about that for a moment. If you take the argument to its full, logical extent, then sex with children and sex with animals also can't be sins because Jesus never explicitly condemned pedophilia or bestiality. The philosophy "Jesus didn't mention it, so it must be okay" is impractical at best and dangerous at worst.

Our good friend Dr. Mark Hitchcock is a fellow writer on our *Tipping Point Prophecy Update* blog, and he shares this about homosexuality:

> Jesus never had to condemn homosexual behavior because it was understood by everyone in the Jewish culture of His day that it was contrary to the Mosaic law (Leviticus 18:22; 20:13).
>
> Second, Jesus frequently referenced Sodom (and a few times, Gomorrah) to warn His listeners of impending doom (Matthew 10:14-15; 11:23-24; Luke 10:10-12; 17:26-30).
>
> The modern English word *sodomy* comes from the homosexual sin of Sodom. Any argument that Jesus supported homosexuality is an argument from silence that disregards His numerous negative references to Sodom.
>
> Additionally, Jesus said the world in the days before His Second Coming will be like the days of Lot in the city of Sodom:
>
> *"It was the same as happened in the days of Lot: they were eating, they were drinking, they were buying, they were selling, they were planting, they were building; but on the day that Lot went out from Sodom it rained fire and brimstone from heaven and destroyed them all. It will be just the same on the day that the Son of Man is revealed."—Luke 17:28-30*

What is happening today in America is no coincidence. It may deeply sadden us but should not surprise us. Jesus told us this would happen as the end draws near.

The Bible must be read cover to cover, and there are zero places in the whole of Scripture where sex between two men or two women is referred to in a positive manner. Instead, we have the story of Sodom where the men of the city demanded to have sex with Lot's male visitors (Genesis 19:1–13). We have the Levitical texts: "You shall not sleep with a male as one sleeps with a female; it is an abomination" and "If *there is* a man who sleeps with a male as those who sleep with a woman, both of them have committed a detestable act" (Leviticus 18:22; 20:13 NASB). We have Paul's letter to the church in Rome: "For this reason God gave them over to degrading passions; for their women exchanged natural relations for that which is contrary to nature, and likewise the men, too, abandoned natural relations with women and burned in their desire toward one another, males with males committing shameful acts and receiving in their own persons the due penalty of their error" (Romans 1:26–27 NASB). And we have two lists from Paul that contain references to homosexuality:

> Or do you not know that the unrighteous will not inherit the kingdom of God? Do not be deceived; neither the sexually immoral, nor idolaters, nor adulterers, nor homosexuals, nor thieves, nor the greedy, nor those habitually drunk, nor verbal abusers, nor swindlers, will inherit the kingdom of God (1 Corinthians 6:9–10 NASB).
>
> We know that the law is good if one uses it properly. We also know that the law is made not for the righteous but for lawbreakers and rebels, the ungodly and sinful, the unholy and irreligious, for those who kill their fathers or mothers, for murderers, for the sexually immoral, for those practicing homosexuality, for slave traders and liars and perjurers—and for whatever else is contrary to the sound doctrine that conforms to the gospel concerning the glory of the blessed God, which he entrusted to me (1 Timothy 1:8–11 NIV).

If we are going to accept adultery in America, we might as well accept homosexuality too, because it is a part of the same sin. If we are going to pick on homosexuals, then we need to pick on adulterers too, because it is all the same in God's mind. We cannot let our favorite sins slide by and pick on the other sinners. That just doesn't work.

Hate isn't the answer for those who are practicing sexual sin. The Bible does not create prejudice—people do. When a woman caught in the act of adultery was brought to Jesus, He told her accusers, "He who is without sin among you, let him throw a stone at her first" (John 8:7). No one could cast the first stone, and Jesus told the woman, "Neither do I condemn you; go and sin no more" (v. 11). Jesus did not condemn this woman, but He also did not condone her sin.

Hate isn't the answer for those who are practicing sexual sin.

The three of us have close relatives who live as homosexuals. In fact, there probably isn't a single lifestyle that is not practiced by someone in our extended family. We love our family, and we will never be hateful toward them or reject them. But we will also not condone their lifestyle. Our prayer is that God will use someone (whether one of us or another person) to tell them the truth and lovingly lead them to Jesus. God is not a hateful, spiteful God. He is merciful, and He wants every person to know the truth and receive His love.

25

The Power of Biblical Meditation

The battlefields of communication, discipline, and sexuality can be filled with twists, turns, and emotional landmines—enough to make any parent want to hide and raise the white flag of surrender. And, of course, those aren't the only parenting challenges today. According to the Pew Research survey we mentioned in the first chapter, parents in the United States are extremely or very worried about these things happening to their children:

- Struggling with anxiety or depression (40 percent)
- Being bullied (35 percent)
- Being kidnapped or abducted (28 percent)
- Getting beaten up or attacked (25 percent)
- Having problems with drugs or alcohol (23 percent)
- Getting shot (22 percent)

Researchers found that "most parents (62 percent) say being a parent has been at least somewhat harder than they expected, with about a quarter (26 percent) saying it's been *a lot* harder."[1]

We didn't have the space to address every parenting challenge in this book. For that, parents must turn to the Bible. Now, to be clear, you won't find modern words like "frenemy" or "gaslighting" in Scripture (at least not in any translation we know of). The

English language is always gaining new words and phrases, but the concepts behind them are not new. Ecclesiastes 1:9 says, "There is nothing new under the sun." Even though we like to think of ourselves as being highly advanced compared to previous generations, we're just dealing with the same problems of pride, greed, anger, bitterness, fear, rejection, loneliness, etc.

Children face all kinds of challenges that bring stress both to them and to their parents, and the key to overcoming these challenges is biblical meditation. This isn't like Eastern or New Age meditation where you clear your mind and focus on yourself or some unknown cosmic power. Rather, biblical meditation is mentally rehearsing Scripture that causes you to think about God and the truth of His Word.

Jimmy's Story

> How can a young man cleanse his way?
> By taking heed according to Your word.
> With my whole heart I have sought You;
> Oh, let me not wander from
> Your commandments!
> Your word I have hidden in my heart,
> That I might not sin against You (Psalm 119:9–11).

After Karen and I got married, I knew the Lord had called me to the ministry, but I was still battling sexual temptation and deception. I wrestled constantly with my thought life and experienced nagging guilt and condemnation because of my inability to stop the thoughts I knew were wrong. I wondered, *How is God ever going to do anything in my life?*

When I was in my mid-twenties, we took a family vacation to Colorado, and I randomly picked up a brown booklet that was lying on the coffee table in the house where we were staying.

It was called *Biblical Meditation: A Transforming Discipline*, by Ronald A. Jensen. The book surprised me—by looking at the cover, I had no idea it talked about pornography, lust, and sexual temptation. The author was a Bible college president who had sold pornography out of his basement as a child and had wrestled with all kinds of lust and sexual temptation for most of his life. He explained how biblical meditation was the only thing that had ever set him free.

Now, I had tried just about everything to be set free sexually. I had tried casting demons out of myself, taking cold showers, removing television from our house, and groveling in repentance to God after every moment of weakness. But nothing worked. I thought to myself, *I might as well try biblical meditation. I don't have anything to lose!*

I had read the Bible on many occasions and studied it diligently as a young Christian, but I had never meditated on Scripture as a practice. As I began, my life was transformed, and the vicious cycle of sexual temptation and defeat ended. I was shocked at how powerful biblical meditation was, and how quickly it worked.

I loaded Scripture into my mind when I read the Bible in the morning. Then I'd keep Scripture in my mind throughout the day. When thoughts of lust, fear, worry, or anxiety would arise, I would replace them at once with God's Word. When you pull out the sword of the Word of God, the enemy knows he is no match.

When you pull out the sword of the Word of God, the enemy knows he is no match.

Over the years, I have walked in sexual victory, but I have never had a season in my life when I wasn't sexually tempted on some level. Biblical meditation does *not* remove the problem forever or guarantee you'll never be tempted again. However, it does offer you an answer to Satan's constant attack against you. When you meditate, you have the power to overcome temptation and sin and experience the victory God promises in His Word.

I wrote a book called *A Mind Set Free: Overcoming Mental Strongholds Through Biblical Meditation.* It's a short, easy-to-read book, and I recommend it to every person who has ever dealt with any kind of problem or temptation. I used to be in terrible bondage, but God's Word set me free. Regardless of how dark your past has been, God invites you into the light of His Word that can heal you, transform you from the inside out, and empower you to live in victory.

Learning to Meditate on God's Word

It is written, "Man shall not live by bread alone, but by every word that proceeds from the mouth of God" (Matthew 4:4).

The word "meditate" as used in the Bible means two basic things: "to consider or ponder" and "to speak or murmur to oneself." A good picture of meditation is an animal that chews its cud and "ruminates." Rumination is the process of chewing, swallowing, and then regurgitating to chew again. A sheep has multiple stomachs, and the process of rumination causes the grass the sheep is eating to be refined over and over until it passes into the final stomach and is digested in a pure form. Likewise, biblical meditation means to take a Bible verse, chapter, or story and put it into your mind. Then, throughout the day, you keep bringing it back into your mind as you keep mentally "chewing on it."

The busiest person in the world can find times throughout the day to meditate. Whether you're on a plane, at the car wash, eating at a restaurant, or lying in bed, you can reflect upon Scripture and enjoy the presence and power of God instantly.

Throughout the day as you face temptations or when you are in a reflective time—sitting at a stoplight, lying in bed, or taking a coffee break at work—bring the Scripture back to mind and pon-der it. Meditation brings God's peace as His Word becomes alive within you and protects your mind against the enemy's attacks.

The presence of God powerfully inhabits His Word. Paul exhorts believers in Ephesians 5:18–19 to continually invite the Holy Spirit's presence into their lives by speaking or "murmuring" to one another with psalms, hymns, and spiritual songs from their hearts to God. A psalm is Scripture put to music, such as the book of Psalms. A hymn is a song about God and any issue concerning God, His kingdom, or an aspect of doctrine. A spiritual song is a new song that you sing personally to God from your own experi-ence and relationship with Him. It is a very intimate sharing of love to God for who He is and for all the things He has done for you.

As you speak and sing psalms, hymns, or spiritual songs, you are meditating. As you do this, the Holy Spirit inhabits your words and praises. The result is a continual flow of the power and peace of God in your life. Truly, speaking and singing to yourself as your focus on God and His Word takes meditation to a higher level. Incorporating this as a habit as you go through your day is a pleasant and practical way to enforce the discipline of biblical meditation.

Promises for Biblical Meditation

God designed every area of your life to operate according to His Word.

God designed every area of your life to operate according to His Word. It is the master instruction manual for humanity. If you want to know how to think, talk, act, or embrace the right ethical or moral point of view, then you will find all those answers in the Bible. But the Bible is not a legalistic book of dos and don'ts. No, it's a book of love.

Then they cried out to the Lord in their trouble,
And He saved them out of their distresses.
He sent His word and healed them,
And delivered *them* from their destructions (Psalm 107:19–20).

If you find yourself struggling with the thought that God doesn't love you, then read Scriptures about God's love. Keep reading them until they get fully digested. If you're struggling with thoughts about condemnation, then read and digest, "There is therefore now no condemnation for those who are in Christ Jesus" (Romans 8:1 ESV). Whatever issue you're struggling with, read what God's Word says about it. This isn't merely a religious exercise; it's deeply practical. Read the Bible, get it deep inside you, and it will come back to you day and night.

The book of Psalms begins with this powerful description of the person who has committed their mind to biblical meditation:

Blessed *is* the man
Who walks not in the counsel of the ungodly,
  Nor stands in the path of sinners,
  Nor sits in the seat of the scornful;
But his delight *is* in the law of the Lord,
And in His law he meditates day and night.
He shall be like a tree
  Planted by the rivers of water,
  That brings forth its fruit in its season,
  Whose leaf also shall not wither;
And whatever he does shall prosper (Psalm 1:1–3).

The power of biblical meditation is so great that God promises everything we do will prosper if we will practice it "day and night." Can you imagine everything in your life prospering? Psalm 1:3 compares a person who meditates on Scripture day and night to a tree planted by a river. The tree doesn't have to worry about whether the rains come because it has a stable source of water to keep it healthy and fruitful. The result is guaranteed success—just as God promises all of us if we will meditate on Scripture.

The times our minds and our children's minds are most open to satanic assault are when we are sitting around our houses (watching TV, scrolling on our phones, etc.); on our way somewhere (listening to music, noticing the person in the car next to us, daydreaming); and lying in bed as we wake up and go to sleep (worrying about our problems, fantasizing about our sinful desires). The devil wants to wear you out by filling your mind with temptation, but when your mind is filled with God's Word, there isn't room for the enemy to come in and mess with you. You do not have to live with regret. You do not have to live in defeat.

Misunderstanding biblical meditation scares most people away. They think it is either impractical or too spiritually difficult for them. The truth is any man, woman, or child can meditate upon Scripture day and night. In the first chapter of this book, we looked at Deuteronomy 6:6–9, which gives parents these instructions:

> And these words which I command you today shall be in your heart. You shall teach them diligently to your children, and shall talk of them when you sit in your house, when you walk by the way, when you lie down, and when you rise up. You shall bind them as a sign on your hand, and they shall be as frontlets between your eyes. You shall write them on the doorposts of your house and on your gates (Deuteronomy 6:6–9).

In these verses, God tells the people of Israel to teach His Word diligently to their children at least four times during the day: when you're on your way somewhere, when you're sitting around your house, when you lie in bed at night, and when you lie in bed in the morning. This is *day and night.* Those times also happen to be the four most meditative times of the day, when our minds go into neutral, and we are the most vulnerable to temptation. God wants His people to meditate on His Word when they have the greatest opportunity to think about it uninterrupted.

When we read God's Word, we load our minds like a powerful weapon. The devil can't come in and attack your mind, because it has already occupied itself with another structure—a house of truth. Remember, you can't take thoughts out of your mind, but you can fill your mind with the right thoughts. If you're battling lust and someone tells you not to lust, then you will lust twice as much. It's the most frustrating thing in the world. You can't take a thought out of your mind, but you can replace it with a greater thought.

You can't take thoughts out of your mind, but you can fill your mind with the right thoughts.

We must remember that the enemy never takes a day off from trying to defraud us of the blessings God has in store for us. Satan will always try to use doubt, fear, condemnation, lies, confusion, deception, and temptation in order to defeat God's people. We don't have to live in fear, though. Instead, we need to remember the apostle Paul's exhortation: "Be strong in the Lord and in his mighty power. Put on all of God's armor so that you will be able to stand firm against all strategies of the devil" (Ephesians 6:10–11 NLT). Every day we must put on the armor of God and fight for victory as we train our children to do the same thing. The Word of God is greater than any weapon of the enemy—it is God's power that works in us when we believe it and confess it. In the worst battle on the worst day of your life, the word of God will save you and set you free.

Epilogue

Is It Too Late?

Having done everything, to stand firm.

—Ephesians 6:13 NASB

Throughout our decades of ministry, we have encountered deeply disheartened parents who asked themselves (and us), *Where did we go wrong? We tried to do what the Bible says regarding our kids, but they are still so lost!* These parents feel intense grief at their failure to bring up godly children. And if they made mistakes—which we *all* do—then they also feel shame. *If only I had done ... If only we had tried ...* The "if onlys" play on a demonic loop, condemning these precious men and women of God.

As the three of us have openly admitted throughout this this book, we are not perfect parents. There simply is no such thing (apart, of course, from our heavenly Father). If you have a child who is not living in obedience to the Lord and you are beating yourself up for it, please hear these words: *it is not your fault.*

We are not saying you didn't make mistakes. We're not saying you couldn't have done better. Some parents make poor choices while others make egregious errors that have a massive influence on their kids' lives. In those situations, we encourage parents to do the only things they can: acknowledge the wrong, repent to God and everyone involved, and do whatever is possible and appropriate to make it right. You cannot change the past, but you can decide not to repeat it.

You cannot change the past, but you can decide not to repeat it.

Still, whether your parenting mistakes were minor or major, every person has a God-given free will. Your child is a person, and they must use this free will to make the choice: serve God or don't serve Him. (By the way, God is a perfect God, and His perfection is not diluted or nullified by a person's rejection of Him. Of course, human parents aren't perfect, but the same idea applies to godly parenting. Ted Tripp explains, "You must do all that God has called you to do, but the outcome is more complex than whether you have done the right things in the right way. Your children are responsible for the way they respond to your parenting."[1])

You can't make the choice for your child, and ultimately, you can't take responsibility for their choice. Ezekiel 18:20 says, "The person who sins is the one who will die. The child will not be punished for the parent's sins, and the parent will not be punished for the child's sins. Righteous people will be rewarded for their own righteous behavior, and wicked people will be punished for their own wickedness" (NLT).

This probably feels very heavy right now, especially if it looks like you've lost the fight for your child's soul. But allow us to share a true story with you that may turn your heartache into hope.

E. M. Bounds was a brilliant man. He finished his law degree at the age of 19 and practiced as an attorney until he felt God's call to the ministry when he was 24. Bounds became a minister and wrote extensively on the topic of prayer until his death in 1913.

One of E. M. Bounds' children was a son named Osborne. Osborne was only 21 years old when his father died. Decades later, when Osborne was 84 years old, a Baptist pastor asked him a surprising question: "Are you a saved man?" Osborne hesitantly replied, "Oh, I don't know. I hope so, but I'm not sure."[2] Obviously, this answer didn't sit well with the pastor, but he also didn't want to badger the elderly gentleman. So the pastor went home, called 12 other pastors, and asked them to join him in praying for Osborne.

The pastor visited again with Osborne several times, but it wasn't until three months after their initial meeting that the pastor was able to present the gospel and asked if Osborne was ready to receive salvation. Osborne instantly agreed. He confessed his sins to the Lord and asked for His forgiveness. After his death, Osborne's daughter told the Baptist pastor, "From the time Daddy talked with you that last time, he had more peace than he ever had before."[3]

Sixty-three years passed after E. M. Bounds's death before his son surrendered his life to Christ. One might think the Christian father died in a state of despair, unsure of the state of his child's soul. But E. M. Bounds believed in prayer, so much so that he wrote the following:

Prayers are deathless. The lips that uttered them may be closed in death, the heart that felt them may have ceased to beat—but the prayers live before God, and God's heart is set on them, and [so] prayers outlive the lives who uttered them; outlive a generation, outlive an age, outlive a world.[4]

Obviously, every parent wants to see their child following God and living for Him. But the ultimate goal of parenting isn't for you to *see it* happen—the ultimate goal is for it to happen!

Your prayers for your child will outlive you. Hebrews 11:1 says, "Now faith is confidence in what we hope for and assurance about what we do not see" (NIV). This chapter of the Bible, full of stories of our biblical heroes, is often referred to as the "Hall of Faith."

All these people died still believing what God had promised them. They did not receive what was promised, but they saw it all from a distance and welcomed it (Hebrews 11:13 NLT).

As American baseball legend Yogi Berra once said, "It ain't over till it's over." It's not too late, dear parents. As long as there is breath in your child's lungs, it isn't too late.

So keep praying. Keeping putting on your spiritual armor and standing firm. Keep fighting for the soul of your child.

Notes

Welcome

1. Carle Zimmerman, *Family and Civilization* (Washington, D.C.: Regnery Publishing, 2008).

2. Amanda Barroso, Kim Parker, and Jesse Bennett, "As Millennials Near 40, They're Approaching Family Life Differently than Previous Generations," Pew Research Center's Social & Demographic Trends Project, May 27, 2020, https://www.pewresearch.org/social-trends/2020/05/27/as-millennials-near-40-theyre-approaching-family-life-differently-than-previous-generations/.

3. Richard Fry and Kim Parker, "Rising Share of U.S. Adults Are Living Without a Spouse or Partner," Pew Research Center's Social & Demographic Trends Project, October 5, 2021, https://www.pewresearch.org/social-trends/2021/10/05/rising-share-of-u-s-adults-are-living-without-a-spouse-or-partner/.

4. Ibid.

5. Stephanie Kramer, "U.S. Has World's Highest Rate of Children Living in Single-Parent Households," Pew Research Center, December 12, 2019, https://www.pewresearch.org/short-reads/2019/12/12/u-s-children-more-likely-than-children-in-other-countries-to-live-with-just-one-parent/.

6. Ibid.

7. Gretchen Livingston, "About One-Third of U.S. Children Are Living with an Unmarried Parent," Pew Research Center, April 27, 2018, https://www.pewresearch.org/short-reads/2018/04/27/about-one-third-of-u-s-children-are-living-with-an-unmarried-parent/

8. The Pew Charitable Trusts, "The Long-Term Decline in Fertility-and What It Means for State Budgets," The Pew Charitable Trusts, December 5, 2022, https://www.pewtrusts.org/en/research-and-analysis

/issue-briefs/2022/12/the-long-term-decline-in-fertility-and-what-it-means-for-state-budgets#:~:text=Forty%2Dthree%20states%20recorded%20their,the%20decade%20ending%20in%202010.

9. Anna Brown, "Growing Share of Childless Adults in U.S. Don't Expect to Ever Have Children," Pew Research Center, November 19, 2021, https://www.pewresearch.org/short-reads/2021/11/19/growing-share-of-childless-adults-in-u-s-dont-expect-to-ever-have-children/.

10. Ibid.

1. The Greater Purpose

1. Rachel Minkin and Juliana Menasce Horowitz, "Parenting in America Today," Pew Research Center's Social & Demographic Trends Project, January 24, 2023, https://www.pewresearch.org/social-trends/2023/01/24/parenting-in-america-today/.

2. Also in Mark 12:30 and Luke 10:27.

3. "Proverbs 22," *Pulpit Commentary* on Bible Hub, accessed May 30, 2023, https://biblehub.com/commentaries/pulpit/proverbs/22.htm.

2. Basic Training

1. "The Importance of Skin-to-Skin with Baby after Delivery," Sanford Health News, June 20, 2023, https://news.sanfordhealth.org/childrens/the-importance-of-skin-to-skin-after-delivery-you-should-know/.

2. Ibid.

3. Melody Whiddon and Marilyn Montgomery, "Is Touch Beyond Infancy Important for Children's Mental Health?" American Counseling Association, 2011, https://www.counseling.org/Resources/Library/VISTAS/2011-V-Online/Article_88.pdf.

4. Sarah Barkley, "What Is Touch Starved? Signs and Tips to Cope," Psych Central, August 2, 2022, https://psychcentral.com/health/ways-to-self-soothe-when-starved-for-touch.

3. The Soul War

1. "5315. Nephesh," Bible Hub, https://biblehub.com/hebrew/5315.htm.

2. "Psuché," *Thayer's Greek Lexicon* on Bible Hub, https://biblehub.com/thayers/5590.htm.

4. Dressed to Kill

1. Garrett Kell, "Tempted and Unarmed: Why We Need the Armor of God," Desiring God, January 18, 2021, https://www.desiringgod.org/articles/tempted-and-unarmed.

2. "222. Alétheia," Bible Hub, https://biblehub.com/greek/225.htm.

3. *Merriam-Webster*, s.v. "truth (*n.*)," accessed May 30, 2023, https://www.merriam-webster.com/dictionary/truth.

4. "Lesson 5: The Shield of Faith," Free Bible Study Guides, accessed May 30, 2023, http://www.freebiblestudyguides.org/bible-teachings/armor-of-god-shield-of-faith.htm.

5. Micheal Chimaobi Kalu, "Centurions and Cohorts: X Facts about the Roman Army," War History Online, March 14, 2019, https://www.warhistoryonline.com/instant-articles/centurions-and-cohorts-10-facts.html?chrome=1.

6. Clarence L. Haynes, "What Is the Helmet of Salvation in the Armor of God?," Christianity.com, August 30, 2022, https://www.christianity.com/wiki/christian-terms/what-is-the-helmet-of-salvation-in-the-armor-of-god.html.

7. "3162. Machaira," Bible Hub, https://biblehub.com/greek/3162.htm

6. Missile Launch

1. "Forgiveness: Your Health Depends on It," Johns Hopkins Medicine, accessed May 30, 2023, https://www.hopkinsmedicine.org/health/wellness-and-prevention/forgiveness-your-health-depends-on-it.

2. "1228. Diabolos," Bible Hub, https://biblehub.com/greek/1228.htm.

7. Free to Fight

1. "5753. Avah," Bible Hub, https://biblehub.com/hebrew/5753.htm.

8. Chain of Command

1. *Merriam-Webster*, s.v. "jealousy (*n.*)," accessed May 30, 2023, https://www.merriam-webster.com/dictionary/jealousy.

9. A Biblical Worldview

1. Cultural Research Center, "Two key questions—What is worldview? What is the biblical worldview?," accessed May 30, 2023, https://www

.arizonachristian.edu/wp-content/uploads/2022/06/CRC-Brief-What-is
-Worldview_Biblical-Worldview_Digital.pdf.

2. Ibid.

3. Ibid.

4. Ibid.

5. George Barna, "American Worldview Inventory 2023 Release #1: Incidence of Biblical Worldview Shows Significant Change Since the Start of the Pandemic," February 28, 2023, Cultural Research Center, https://www.arizonachristian.edu/wp-content/uploads/2023/02/CRC_AWVI2023_Release1.pdf.

6. Ibid.

7. George Barna, "American Worldview Inventory 2022 Release #4: Improving Parents' Ability to Raise Spiritual Champions," April 22, 2022, Cultural Research Center, https://www.arizonachristian.edu/wp-content/uploads/2022/04/AWVI2022_Release_04_Digital.pdf.

8. George Barna, "American Worldview Inventory 2022 Release #2: The Strengths and Weaknesses of What Pre-Teen Parents Believe and Do," March 29, 2022, Cultural Research Center, https://www.arizonachristian.edu/wp-content/uploads/2022/03/AWVI2022_Release_02_Digital.pdf.

9. Tedd Tripp, *Shepherding a Child's Heart* (Wapwallopen, PA: Shepherd Press, 2005), 52–53.

10. See www.ourbibleapp.com.

10. Who Am I?

1. See John Beeson, "Why the Bible Calls Women 'Sons of God,'" Preach It, Teach It, accessed May 30, 2023, https://preachitteachit.org/articles/detail/why-the-bible-calls-women-sons-of-god/.

2. Brittany Yesudasan, "Your Identity in Christ: How God Sees You," Cru.org, accessed June 16, 2022, https://www.cru.org/us/en/train-and-grow/spiritual-growth/core-christian-beliefs/identity-in-christ.html.

3. "What Is Speciesism?" PETA, February 10, 2020, https://www.peta.org/about-peta/faq/what-is-speciesism/.

11. United We Stand

1. *Merriam-Webster*, s.v. "close *(v.)*," accessed May 30, 2023, https://www.merriam-webster.com/dictionary/close.

12. Joining Ranks

1. "Stepfamily Statistics," The Stepfamily Foundation, accessed May 30, 2023, https://www.stepfamily.org/stepfamily-statistics.html.
2. Scott and Vanessa Martindale, *Blended and Redeemed* (Southlake, TX: XO Publishing, 2022), 270–71.
3. Martindale, *Blended and Redeemed*, 260.

14. Gatekeeper

1. Pixalate, "Pixalate's Harris Poll Survey Recap: Children's Privacy in Mobile Apps," Pixalate, March 1, 2022, https://www.pixalate.com/blog/childrens-online-privacy-harris-poll-recap.
2. Sarah Novicoff and Matthew A. Kraft, "The Potential Role of Instructional Time in Pandemic Recovery," Brookings, November 15, 2022, https://www.brookings.edu/blog/brown-center-chalkboard/2022/11/15/the-potential-role-of-instructional-time-in-pandemic-recovery/.

15. Training Maneuvers

1. "How Parents Used Their Time in 2021," U.S. Bureau of Labor Statistics, July 22, 2022, https://www.bls.gov/opub/ted/2022/how-parents-used-their-time-in-2021.htm.
2. Gretchen Livingston and Kim Parker, "8 Facts about American Dads," Pew Research Center, June 12, 2019, https://www.pewresearch.org/short-reads/2019/06/12/fathers-day-facts/.
3. Marie Haaland, "Parents Only Spend 24 Minutes More with Their Kids than They Do Their Phones, Study Finds," digitalhub US, September 6, 2021, https://swnsdigital.com/us/2019/10/parents-only-spend-24-minutes-more-with-their-kids-than-they-do-their-phones-study-finds/.

16. The War for Words

1. "Facts about Suicide," Centers for Disease Control and Prevention, May 2023, https://www.cdc.gov/suicide/facts/index.html.

18. The Discipline Battle

1. Naaz Modan and Kara Arundel, "School Shootings Reach Unprecedented High in 2022," K-12 Dive, December 21, 2022, https://www.k12dive.com/news/2022-worst-year-for-school-shootings/639313/.

22. Shameless Sexuality

1. John Fort, "Are You Afraid to Talk to Your Kids about Sex?" XXXchurch.com, November 17, 2022, https://xxxchurch.com/parents/are-you-afraid-to-talk-to-your-kids-about-sex.html.

2. Veronica Zambon, "Types of Gender Identity: Types and Definitions," Medical News Today, January 3, 2023, https://www.medicalnewstoday.com/articles/types-of-gender-identity#fa-qs.

3. Walt Heyer, "Transgender Regret Is Real Even If the Media Says Otherwise," The Federalist, August 19, 2015, https://thefederalist.com/2015/08/19/transgender-regret-is-real-even-if-the-media-tell-you-otherwise/.

4. Kevin DeYoung, "What Does the Bible Say about Transgenderism?," The Gospel Coalition, September 8, 2016, https://www.thegospelcoalition.org/blogs/kevin-deyoung/what-does-the-bible-say-about-transgenderism/.

5. Mandy Majors, *Keeping Children Safe in a Digital World: A Solution That Works* (Coppell, TX: Mandy Majors), 33.

6. Majors, *Keeping Children Safe in a Digital World*, 54–55.

23. Lies About Sex, Part 1

1. Nicholas Wolfinger, "Does Sexual History Affect Marital Happiness?," Institute for Family Studies, October 22, 2018, https://ifstudies.org/blog/does-sexual-history-affect-marital-happiness.

2. Nikki Graf, "Key Findings on Marriage and Cohabitation in the U.S.," Pew Research Center, November 6, 2019, https://www.pewresearch.org/short-reads/2019/11/06/key-findings-on-marriage-and-cohabitation-in-the-u-s/.

3. Theresa E. DiDonato, "Are Couples That Live Together before Marriage More Likely to Divorce?," Psychology Today, January 27, 2021, https://www.psychologytoday.com/us/blog/meet-catch-and-keep/202101/is-living-together-marriage-associated-divorce.

4. "Top Websites Ranking," Similarweb, accessed June 12, 2023, https://www.similarweb.com/top-websites/.

5. "Porn Industry Revenue – Numbers & Stats," Bedbible Research Center, January 13, 2023, https://bedbible.com/porn-industry-revenue-statistics/

6. Josh McDowell, *The Porn Phenomenon: The Impact of Pornography in the Digital Age* (Ventura, CA: Barna Group, 2016), 22.

7. Fight the New Drug, "How Porn Can Normalize Sexual Objectification," Fight the New Drug, accessed June 12, 2023, https://fightthenewdrug.org

/how-porn-can-normalize-sexual-objectification/; Sarah J. Gervais and Sarah Eagan, "Sexual Objectification: The Common Thread Connecting Myriad Forms of Sexual Violence against Women.," *American Journal of Orthopsychiatry* 87, no. 3 (2017): 226–32, https://doi.org/10.1037/ort0000257.

8. Fight the New Drug; Yanyan Zhou et al., "Pornography Use, Two Forms of Dehumanization, and Sexual Aggression: Attitudes vs. Behaviors," *Journal of Sex & Marital Therapy* 47, no. 6 (2021): 571–90, https://doi.org/10.1080/0092623x.2021.1923598; Renee Mikorski and Dawn M. Szymanski, "Masculine Norms, Peer Group, Pornography, Facebook, and Men's Sexual Objectification of Women," *Psychology of Men & Masculinity* 18, no. 4 (2017): 257–67, https://doi.org/10.1037/men0000058; M. N. Skorska, G. Hodson, and M. R. Hoffarth, "Experimental Effects of Degrading versus Erotic Pornography Exposure in Men on Reactions toward Women (Objectification, Sexism, Discrimination)," *The Canadian Journal of Human Sexuality* 27 (2018): 261–76.

9. Fight the New Drug; John D. Foubert, Matthew W. Brosi, and R. Sean Bannon, "Pornography Viewing among Fraternity Men: Effects on Bystander Intervention, Rape Myth Acceptance and Behavioral Intent to Commit Sexual Assault," *Sexual Addiction & Compulsivity* 18, no. 4 (2011): 212–31, https://doi.org/10.1080/10720162.2011.625552.

10. Fight the New Drug; Foubert, Brosi, and Bannon, "Pornography Viewing among Fraternity Men"; John D. Foubert and Ana J. Bridges, "What Is the Attraction? Pornography Use Motives in Relation to Bystander Intervention," *Journal of Interpersonal Violence* 32, no. 20 (2016): 3071–89, https://doi.org/10.1177/0886260515596538.

11. Fight the New Drug; Foubert, Brosi, and Bannon, "Pornography Viewing among Fraternity Men"; Steve Loughnan et al., "Sexual Objectification Increases Rape Victim Blame and Decreases Perceived Suffering," *Psychology of Women Quarterly* 37, no. 4 (2013): 455–61, https://doi.org/10.1177/0361684313485718.

12. Fight the New Drug; Paul J. Wright and Robert S. Tokunaga, "Men's Objectifying Media Consumption, Objectification of Women, and Attitudes Supportive of Violence against Women," *Archives of Sexual Behavior* 45, no. 4 (2015): 955–64, https://doi.org/10.1007/s10508-015-0644-8.; Rita C. Seabrook, L. Monique Ward, and Soraya Giaccardi, "Less than Human? Media Use, Objectification of Women, and Men's Acceptance of Sexual Aggression," *Psychology of Violence* 9, no. 5 (2019): 536–45, https://doi.org/10.1037/vio0000198.

13. Fight the New Drug; Johanna M. van Oosten and Laura Vandenbosch, "Predicting the Willingness to Engage in Non-Consensual Forwarding of Sexts: The Role of Pornography and Instrumental Notions of Sex," *Archives of Sexual Behavior* 49, no. 4 (2020): 1121–32, https://doi.org/10.1007/s10508-019-01580-2.

14. Fight the New Drug; Paul J. Wright, Robert S. Tokunaga, and Ashley Kraus, "A Meta-Analysis of Pornography Consumption and Actual Acts of Sexual Aggression in General Population Studies," *Journal of Communication* 66, no. 1 (February 2016): 183–205, https://doi.org/10.1111/jcom.12201; Whitney L. Rostad et al., "The Association between Exposure to Violent Pornography and Teen Dating Violence in Grade 10 High School Students," *Archives of Sexual Behavior* 48, no. 7 (2019): 2137–47, https://doi.org/10.1007/s10508-019-1435-4; Amanda Goodson, Cortney A. Franklin, and Leana A. Bouffard, "Male Peer Support and Sexual Assault: The Relation between High-Profile, High School Sports Participation and Sexually Predatory Behaviour," *Journal of Sexual Aggression* 27, no. 1 (2020): 64–80, https://doi.org/10.1080/13552600.2020.1733111; Mikorski and Szymanski, "Masculine Norms, Peer Group, Pornography, Facebook," 257–67.

15. "Masturbation Definition & Meaning," Dictionary.com, accessed June 12, 2023, https://www.dictionary.com/browse/masturbation.

16. Mandy Majors, *TALK: A Practical Approach to Cyberparenting and Open Communication* (Coppell, TX: Mandy Majors, 2017), 209.

17. Majors, *TALK*, 209.

18. Majors, *TALK*, 209–210.

24. Lies About Sex, Part 2

1. Matthew Saxey, "Do 'Church Ladies' Really Have Better Sex Lives?," Institute for Family Studies, November 16, 2020, https://ifstudies.org/blog/do-church-ladies-really-have-better-sex-lives.

2. Stephen Cranney, "The Influence of Religiosity/Spirituality on Sex Life Satisfaction and Sexual Frequency: Insights from the Baylor Religion Survey," *Review of Religious Research* 62, no. 2 (2020): 289–314, https://doi.org/10.1007/s13644-019-00395-w.

3. "Sexually Transmitted Infections (STIs)," World Health Organization, August 22, 2022, https://www.who.int/news-room/fact-sheets/detail/sexually-transmitted-infections-(stis) .

4. Adrienne Santos-Longhurst, "The One Difference Between STIs and STDs—and How to Minimize Your Risk," Healthline, September 9, 2020, https://www.healthline.com/health/healthy-sex/sti-vs-std.

5. "Sexually Transmitted Infections (STIs)."

6. International Planned Parenthood Federation, *Sexual rights: An IPPF Declaration*, October 2008, https://www.ippf.org/sites/default/files /sexualrightsippfdeclaration_1.pdf.

7. Gabrielle Kassel, "What Does It Actually Mean to Be 'Sex Positive'?," Healthline, September 3, 2020, https://www.healthline.com/health /healthy-sex/sex-positive-meaning.

8. Kassel, "What Does it Actually Mean."

25. The Power of Biblical Meditation

1. Minkin and Horowitz, "Parenting in America Today."

Epilogue: Is It Too Late?

1. Tripp, *Shepherding a Child's Heart*, 16.

2. Marion H. Price, Sr., *Never Quit Praying for Your Loved Ones* (Asheville, NC: Revival Literature, 1998), 6.

3. Price, *Never Quit Praying*, 11.

4. E. M. Bounds, *E. M. Bounds on Prayer* (Peabody, MA: Hendrickson Publishers, Inc., 2006), 172.

MORE FROM JIMMY & KAREN EVANS

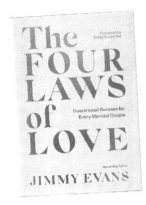

The Four Laws of Love

Jimmy Evans outlines the foundational pillars upon which God designed marriage. He tells the story of his own marriage, which was hurtling toward divorce, until he recognized and put into practice these four laws.

ISBN: 978-1-950113-19-4
Also available in eBook and audiobook

Vision Retreat Guidebook

Serving as a hands-on, practical tool, the information contained in this journal will lead you to address important topics such as spiritual and personal growth, marriage priorities and values, establishing a vision for your family, and much more.

ISBN: 978-1-950113-59-0
Also available in eBook

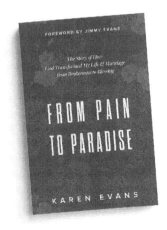

From Pain to Paradise

Karen Evans takes you on an autobiographical journey through the hurts of her past. Through her testimony, she'll show you how to restore relationships, heal broken marriages, and gain victory over emotional pain through the power of the Word of God.

ISBN: 978-0-9600831-2-1
Also available in eBook

You can find these Jimmy & Karen Evans resources and more at store.xomarriage.com or wherever books are sold.
For wholesale pricing, email sales@xomarriage.com.

 **NOW**